2450

THE SERIALS COLLECTION

CURRENT ISSUES IN SERIALS MANAGEMENT

Number one: The Serials Collection: Organization and Administration

Number two: Union Lists: Issues and Answers

Number three: Serials Collection Development: Choices and Strategies

THE SERIALS COLLECTION:
ORGANIZATION AND ADMINISTRATION

edited by
Nancy Jean Melin

Serials Librarian
Graduate School and University Center
City University of New York

THE PIERIAN PRESS
1982

Library of Congress Catalog Card Number 82-81133
ISBN 0-87650-140-4

Copyright © 1982, The Pierian Press
All Rights Reserved

THE PIERIAN PRESS
P.O. Box 1808
Ann Arbor, MI. 48106

Contents

Introduction vii

Serials Organization in Academic Libraries:
   Is There a Best Way? 1
  William Hepfer

Interplay – The Technical and Public Aspects of Serials 9
  Richard J. Behles

Serials: Separate or Merged? 15
  Jennifer Cargill

The Role of the Central Serials Unit
   in an Automated Library 23
  Mitsuko Collver

Serials Staffing Guidelines for the 80's 35
  Margaret McKinley

AACR2 and Serial Records 53
  Wilma Reid Cipolla

The Central Serial Record at New York Public Library:
   An Analysis and a Survey 67
  Minna C. Saxe

Serials Automation: Four Years Later 79
  John Riddick

Popular Serials 83
  Michael H. Randall

Managing and Building a Newspaper Collection 91
  Linda Ervin

Computerized Management of Microforms 103
  Nancy Patricia O'Brien

Government Publications As Serials 115
  Steven D. Zink

**Little Magazines in Special Collections and
    Rare Book Departments** 127
  Cristine C. Rom

**The Exchange of Publications: An Alternative
    to Acquisitions** 151
  Pamela Bluh and Virginia C. Haines

Contributors 159

INTRODUCTION

This is the first publication in a series dedicated to the special problems of managing serials in libraries. The scope of projected contributions to the series includes materials on staff organization and administration, union listing work, serials automation, and collection organization, management, and development.

In this initial volume, specialists have addressed major issues confronting serials managers today. Increasing automation in Technical Services has forced a reappraisal of traditional organizational patterns. Five authors discuss the problem of whether organization by format or function is a preferred choice. Their experiences are varied and it is no surprise that they do not reach a single conclusion.

Other authors consider the importance of AACR2 on serial records, the work of inventorying records and collections in preparation for automating serials, and, the impact of an automated serials check-in system on technical and public services after a four year period.

The remaining six essays address special types of serials including newspapers, popular magazines, microforms, government publications, little magazines, and exchange journals and series. These materials have traditionally been recognized as special problems in libraries where they have not been separated into special departments or collections.

Issues relating to serials management remain constant ones. While the volume was planned to identify and address current issues, serials specialists will find this volume valuable as a reflection of concerns discussed in serials literature over the years as well as a useful guide for planning serials organization and management activities for years to come.

Nancy Jean Melin

SERIALS ORGANIZATION IN ACADEMIC LIBRARIES: IS THERE A BEST WAY?

William Hepfer

Consider the following statements:
1. A serial is a serial is a serial.
2. Acquisitions is acquisitions is acquisitions.
3. Cataloging is cataloging is cataloging.

Respond:
A. One of the above statements is true.
B. Two of the above statements are true.
C. All three statements are true.

Each of these three responses will evoke strong support from a sizeable segment of the academic library community. Response "A" would find adherents in a group which would only accept number one as gospel and discount the others. This vocal throng believes that serials are so unique that they *must* be handled separately from other library operations, the rest of technical services be damned.

Responses "B" and "C," on the other hand, would find favor with those who believe that everything and anything can be accommodated within the traditional administrative arrangement of technical services: two departments handling all aspects of acquisitions and cataloging respectively. Advocates of "B" would swear that only numbers two and three are true; a serial, to them, is nothing more than one of several bibliographic formats which should be acquired and cataloged within the most uniform workflow possible.

"C" respondees are a more flexible crowd. They would agree that serials have certain unique characteristics which entitle them to specialized handling, but they do not regard this as just cause for establishing a separate department within technical services.

Each of these points of view is not without its pros and cons which will vary in proportion depending on numerous circumstances. Some factors are analyzable in terms of organizational principles, while others are solely influenced by external situations.

Figure 1

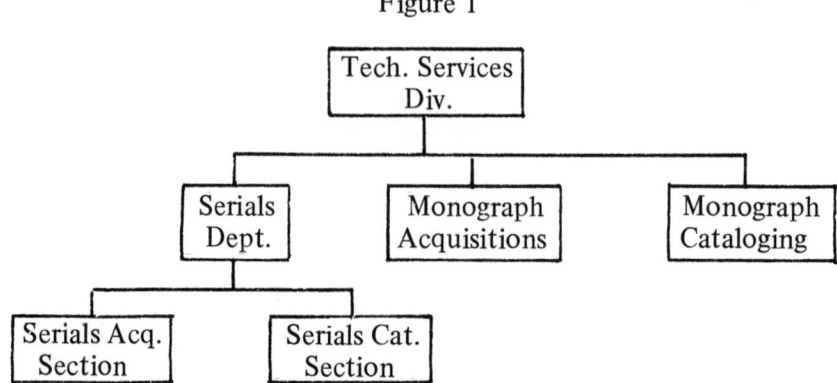

Figure 1 shows a generalized organization chart representing the preference of those who voted for Response A. It requires three department heads whose responsibilities are clearly defined by form *and* function. Serials are treated discretely in such an arrangement, and serials department personnel would devote all of their energies to ordering, receiving, and processing publications which aspire to live forever. Likewise, monograph acquisitions and cataloging personnel would tend exclusively to their respective areas of single-title format specialization.

More articles have appeared in the past 50 years supporting the creation of separate serials departments than any other arrangement. Of course this might be because the traditional monographs/serials acquisitions/cataloging scheme is so established that it doesn't need to justify its existence and because the purely functional approach is still too new a concept to attract much of a following.

Many reasons for serials departmentalization have been argued by many people. Gable first espoused such an arrangement in 1935 when he predicted that "a complete division of book and serial functions will ultimately become necessary . . . I therefore advise the reorganization of serial work within the library to collect all serial functions under one head."[1] This was a rather radical departure from accepted practice at the time, but Gable found support a few years later when Rothman and Ditzion recommended that "complete centralization of functions relating to serials offers the best solution to vexing problems."[2]

Brown contends that "Serials do not fit easily into the other routines of the library. At least acquiring them and keeping them coming require different approaches. They are very individual. Their eccentricities are more easily kept under control in a freedom established within their own Department."[3]

This notion is supported by Weber who says, "The processing of like materials such as serials has been found to be a very successful way to ease the flow of this particularly difficult form. The difficulty stems from the continual changeability of serials and thus the need to constantly be on top of the work flow."[4]

Serials departmentalization, according to Gable, would provide a distinct measure of economy for the library for the following reasons: (1) the work may be more easily and efficiently done where the records are kept, (2) the work may be done by trained serials workers, (3) the evil of over-departmentalization can not appear, (4) there is no unnecessary duplication of records, (5) the same persons handle all the necessary records, thus eliminating possibility of error or duplication of material, and (6) the service to the public is greatly improved.[5]

Although Gable may understate the virtue of having a staff trained to cope specifically with serials, Weber is quite vociferous on this point. He contends that serials staff members "know serials inside and out and understand the problems and vagaries of this form. Such an attitude goes far toward a much more efficient processing work flow and a substantial decrease in a natural reluctance to put aside an unfamiliar form that "outsiders" usually associate with nothing but unpleasant problems."[6]

Few monograph-related problems rival the perplexity caused by serials publications which unexpectedly change title, frequency, or source. Mergers, splits, supplements, and indefinite suspensions can be even more frustrating. They are not unusual within serials operations, however, and a trained staff will handle them in stride. "This basic attitude of normality for sometimes so "abnormal" a form is the underlying strength of a unit that is structured to handle exclusively this type of material."[7]

Collver's research is based on applying management science principles to library operations to determine the most productive ways of grouping technical services. She indicates that monograph and serial workflow are vastly different and should be kept separate. Whereas monograph procedures are sequential (work flows from A to B but not from B to A), serials activities are repeated during the lifetime of these ongoing publications. "[Serials] work is done by interaction, and no function can continue for long without reactions from other activities . . . . Thus, . . . all serials-related activities should be grouped into one unit for the benefit of maximum coordination."[8]

Are these reasons for establishing a separate serials department so strong that other points of view are not worth consideration? Are they based on undeniable truths, or are they somewhat less than models of objectivity? It does not take much cross-examination to discover that most of the arguments are somewhat prejudiced because serials have been accorded a questionable elite status by those who work exclusively with these troublesome publications.

While monograph-oriented librarians might not wholly concur, neither do they challenge the serials separatists because they themselves have stigmatized serials and prefer not to be bothered by them. Weber acknowledges that

> a factor that is often overlooked in the differences in processing books and serials is that there is often a strong negative psychological attitude toward serials in major units that are primarily book-oriented. While this statement may seem somewhat paranoid, it is a fact that the mostly one-time processing of monographic materials leaves a sense of immediate accomplishment in a task that can be seen to be finished and not of continuing duration.[9]

Figure 2

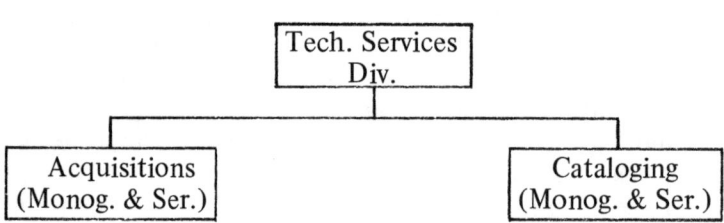

Truly creative librarians will not reject the organizational scheme shown in Figure 2 without giving it fair consideration. In this kind of arrangement, the staff is charged to acquire and catalog all authorized items regardless of format. Monographs and serials travel the same route here, and staff members are expected to handle either type of publication with equal proficiency. Gorman advocated this approach at the Milwaukee conference on serials automation in 1980.[10] According to Gorman, separate serials and book units should be eliminated, and all processing – ordering, receiving, and cataloging – should be organized by function.

Whether the organization chart in Figure 2 is practicable for any given academic library depends on how much credence one grants the "serials *are* different" philosophy. No one can argue that there are no differences, or that the differences should be ignored. Rather, the question becomes whether the technical services staff can be effectively trained to cope with the differences – to understand how and why serials and monographs differ and to fathom the innumerable bibliographic quirks toward which both are inclined.

Such an undertaking should be possible if personnel are handled with sensitivity, and if they are not deluged with an overwhelming amount of detail. Book or serial-oriented staff members may feel threatened at first because they fear that their existing expertise will become ineffectual if it is diluted with too much additional information. This is partly legitimate of course — people can absorb only so much detail — but many persons simply need to be reassured that there is nothing sacred about either format. Indeed, in small libraries, it is not uncommon to have one person responsible for all acquisition work and another doing all of the cataloging.

Perhaps organization by function is an idea whose time has come because all libraries are looking for ways to streamline their operations. Any idea which aspires to offer greater efficiency and lower costs, however, must be carefully planned. Nothing should be left to chance because the frustration of a staff with unclear responsibilities will doom any scheme before it has a chance to demonstrate its real worth.

Many libraries have already tried functional reorganization, but it is still too early to fully assess the strengths and weakness of this arrangement.

McKinley, meanwhile, laments that "Function has to all appearances triumphed over form and serials specialists are encouraged to seek new career paths."[11] She contends that these specialists will not disappear, however, because, even if they are not part of the formal organizational structure, they will evolve due to naturally emergent communication patterns. Experienced specialists

> "are necessary to the efficient operation of a serials processing network and . . . they will work best if they can do so within the established organizational structure. If this support is denied, library planners should anticipate the development of an unpredictable communication system outside the organizational framework and should hope that it will meet their stated objectives."[12]

The more traditional technical services arrangement shown in Figure 3 has proved to be effective in a large number of academic libraries. Given a feasible setting, it offers most of the advantages that have already been attributed to separate serials departments. It accomplishes the same ends with one less department head. Unless the collection is so large and the attendant problems are so many that only two department heads are unable to manage processing activities, this should not present difficulties given a proper climate of management.

Any library department with more than a temporary serials backlog is understaffed or needs to be reorganized. Departments which fall victim to this kind of false economy cannot provide the

Figure 3

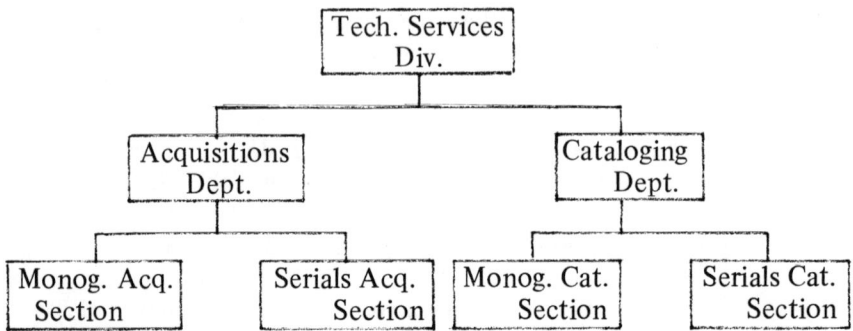

current attention that serials demand, and they will suffer doubly in the end.

How many serials-related problems a library will face depends on a wide variety of circumstances. The number of titles in the collection is certainly a critical factor, but so is the concomitant complexity of the titles involved. Academic libraries which acquire and catalog more than a few foreign language periodicals, conference proceedings, loose-leaf services, and monographic series will need a staff with advanced bibliographic skills to handle the problems which invariably accompany these special publications.

Bibliographic skills pertaining to serials are partially trainable, but there is a much higher level of capability which comes only from experience. This kind of experience comes from applying the knowledge and intuition gained in one situation to a similar situation which follows. Such a learning process will be enhanced by specialization because an employee is more likely to encounter a similar situation if he is working with the same format on a regular basis.

Weber suggests that smaller academic libraries (e.g., a college library serving 1,000 to 2,000 students) may find that it would require too much of their limited staff to collect some of their forms into separate units (e.g., serials, documents). However, "there comes a point . . . when the *size* of the institution — and this usually translates into greater processing loads as the institution's programs grow or are already in the 5,000 item range for active subscriptions — make it really necessary to consolidate certain factors by form for optimum efficiency."[13]

Conclusion

There is not a single scheme for organizing technical services which is ideal for all libraries. The complexity of the collection is the most important determinant as to whether serials specialization is really as sacrosanct as Gable, Brown and the others have contended.

Although only three stylized organization schemes have been discussed here, several other arrangements are possible just by manipulating the boxes in the three illustrations. (To be sure, many libraries have a single unit handling all acquisitions and only specialize by format within the cataloging department.) The configurations become almost limitless when one adds subdivisions such as preorder searching, bindery preparations, invoice payment and claiming.

Reorganization is not a project to be undertaken lightly. The "Let's try something different for a week and see what happens" approach seldom works because, without proper planning, chaos is inevitable. Organizational planning must anticipate all conceivable setbacks including such seemingly unrelated problems as architectural constraints and staff capability. These circumstances are nonetheless real and, although few have true permanence, they should not be ignored. The perceived gains might turn out to be costlier than the existing arrangement if just a few obstacles are overlooked in the planning stage.

NOTES

1. Gable, J. Harris. "The New Serials Department," *Library Journal* 60 (1935), p. 870.

2. Rothman, Fred B. and Sidney Ditzion. "Prevailing Practices in Handling Serials." *College and Research Libraries* 1 (1940), p. 169.

3. Brown, Clara D. and Lynn S. Smith. *Serials, Past, Present, and Future*, 2d (rev.) ed. (Birmingham, AL: Ebsco Industries, 1980), p. 20-21.

4. Weber, Hans H. "Serials Administration." (*Serials Librarian* 4 (1979), p. 144.

5. Gable. p. 870.

6. Weber. p. 144.

7. Weber. p44.

8. Collver, Mitsuko. "Organization of Serials Work for Manual and Automated Systems." *Library Resources & Technical Services* 24 (1980), p. 310.

9. Weber, p. 147.

10. Gorman, Michael. Speaking at the conference on "Serials Automation: Acquisitions and Inventory Control," in Milwaukee, September 5, 1980.

11. McKinley, Margaret M. "Serials Departments: Doomed to Extinction." *Serials Librarian* 5 (1980), p. 15.

12. McKinley, p. 24.

13. Weber, p. 148.

INTERPLAY – THE TECHNICAL AND PUBLIC ASPECTS OF SERIALS

Richard J. Behles

The work of the serials department is not easily categorized. It would seem that there is an abundance of serials meetings, workshops, sessions, and other gatherings sponsored by numerous groups which may be devoted either to public services or to technical services. Most public services people would tend to define serialists strictly in terms of their "back room" processing responsibilities. And technical services groups too often limit their focus to the issues of the cataloging sphere. The work of the serials department, with its concentration on processing activities, has as its broader purpose, public delivery of a very special product, a product which accordingly carries very special interpretive problems. In short, the serials department, while falling between the two stools, really finds its seat in both camps.

The technical processing aspects of serials work are all too obvious. Even if we omit the stages of cataloging and classification and concentrate on a purely alphabetized serials collection, the nature of so much of the department's work remains as processing work. The massive routine of check-in, claiming, binding, and paying invoices is what constitutes the hub of the serials wheel.

It is this truth that invites the use of the ever-denigrating term "clerical" to describe these activities. Let us instead suggest the word "documentational" as a more appropriate descriptor. In its most stripped-down state, the function of serials work is a highly specialized form of record-keeping, a "documenting" effort. Its degree of specialization becomes clear when we consider that the language of volumes, issue numbers, binding specifications, and other elements, constitutes a very unique kind of code, the mastery of which requires care, educated judgment, and a disciplined attention to close details. Accordingly, the daily arranging of this muddle requires an individual of true professional calibre to ensure that the maintenance of this problematic material is of the highest quality. It does take certain polished skills to perfect this maintenance in the constant quest for accurate documentation. And there are many examples of times when the lack of professionalism in the nuts-and-bolts arena has spelled certain disaster at the public delivery point.

Efficient Delivery of Information

It is this public delivery that is the *raison d'etre* of the serials processing work. As easy as it is to become preoccupied with mechanical procedures, it is vital for serials personnel to realize fully the very reason for those procedures. The serials staff must never overlook the fact that the materials at hand (regardless of all their gross tonnage) are all items that are hopefully to be found and used. The end result of all their documentational efforts is, and always will be, efficient information delivery. A truly accurate and efficient serials assistant is a vital member of the professional information team.

It is due to the troublesome nature of serials that this professional efficiency carries such significance. The lengthy accounts of title changes, subscription lags, format changes, erratic numberings, and a host of other complications, have reared their ugly heads frequently throughout the literature. Serialists know fully well that they can expect just about any variety of bibliographic stumbling block to present itself. It is well known that the worst of these expectations manage to materialize all too often.

Perhaps the single most important talent that the serials assistant brings to this confusion is the consistent ability to address and sort fine details. As is true for our sister technical service of cataloging, the very essence of the job lies in these fine bits of bibliographic data. Indeed, they are sometimes enough to turn many people away quickly and sourly. And surely, not everyone is equipped to confront and conquer them.

And so, assistance in interpreting serials bibliographics is essential. A great part of the serialist's importance lies in educating others to develop the trained eye. This guidance reaches both the general public of library users and the other members of the library staff who must in some way experience contact with serials. It is not at all uncommon for the serials staff to have direct contact with the using public during times of shelving or gathering completed current volumes. In these cases, the back-room technical assistant has become an extension of the reference desk, and must add the customary personableness and courtesy associated with good reference work to established technical expertise. Let us never forget that all the painstaking efforts of documentation exist exclusively for the purpose of providing quality personal attention.

> Adequate records are of course necessary for precisely the purpose . . . of keeping library users informed of the

missing parts of current periodicals and the reasons for it.[1]

Perhaps even more important, however, is the briefing of the reference staff. There are possibly as many methods and techniques in handling serials as there are serials in existence. Every library, and every type of library, has its particular system or subsystem for treating its serials, essentially dictated by the overall objectives of its collection development and retention policies. This means that prior reference experience with other serials arrangements needs to be supplemented with an extensive program to acquaint the reference workers with the particular idiosyncrasies of each library's serials handling system.

The importance of this briefing cannot be overemphasized in light of the great proportion of reference queries that have to do with serials. With the increasing reliance upon serial literature in nearly all disciplines, and with the greatly improved means of electronic access to citations, it is no wonder that reference workers are seeing more and more requests for verification of serials titles, in addition to requests for lost, missing, or otherwise problem volumes. More and more, the serials collection is demonstrating its own prominence right at the point of public contact.

This increased demand logically brings with it an inescapable demand globally. Resource sharing activities are well beyond the mere lip service stage, and requests for journals have left their mark on interlibrary loan as well. And this in turn means that the serials staff must bear in mind an extended using public, beyond the walls of the home library. All the technical mechanics must be readily adaptable for participation in external projects.

Reference Functions and Serials

Further, reference workers' contact with serials is even more inherent. So much of the reference collection consists of serial materials, from indices and abstracts, to other less obvious examples like certain yearbooks and handbooks. So the reference staff has under its own jurisdiction many cases of potential serials problems. Consequently, it is inescapable that the reference staff must frequently confer with serials personnel regarding the usual questions of subscription status, volume integrity, bindery specifications, and the like. Even despite the more glamorous advances in automation, printed indices and abstracts still are, and will continue to remain, important items. In difficult economic times, automation is not feasible for everyone, nor is it exclusively applicable for all types of searches. Consequently, reference staffs will always have some subscriptions problems with which to contend.

The reference librarians make extensive use of serials in

their work, and we try to cooperate with them in every way possible, sometimes adapting our usual routines to fit their needs better.[2]

As mentioned previously, there is also much call for interaction directly with the using public. Obviously, the real worth of any serials collection appears in the use made of it. Some type of statistical use-measuring device is highly beneficial in observing this. In open collections, this can be difficult due to the eagerness of those patrons willing to re-shelve their own materials; however, designated return carts and tables do help to encourage public cooperation. It is good practice to monitor the use regularly, even if recording specific pieces used may occur only at selected times. Studies of this kind not only indicate strong subjects and titles, but also provide an overall survey of general usage volume, a significant point to consider in allocating support for serials personnel and materials.

Use Studies and Collection Development

The head of the serials department will find further value in statistical studies when applying them to the selection/acquisitions process. In the academic library, they are an exceptional source of guidance when negotiating collection development strategy with faculty. At times, they may even startle some faculty members who surprisingly discover that their students have not actually been using the materials. Fortunately, this often leads to increased programs of bibliographic instruction and orientation to search strategies. All in all, usage studies provide a good basis for public contact with faculty.

In addition, the serials head must turn to the tools of public service such as indexes, abstracts, and union lists for similar guidance in selection. Accurate and reliable union lists play an increasingly larger part in this work in light of our observations on resource sharing.

One very practical way of keeping familiar with these reference tools is for the serials manager to share occasional responsibility on the reference desk. It is especially worthwhile to remain close to the A&I sources, since coverage changes so rapidly in response to the burgeoning serials population. The reference desk is the best place to keep abreast of titles in demand, and this contact with the sources helps in anticipating that demand. Additionally, this reference work enables the serials specialist to experience first-hand the mechanics of journal citations, especially in terms of how they should relate to bindery specifications. After all, a complete and accurate citation means nothing when a patron must confront a poorly-designed scheme of confusing spines. The logic of what appears on the volume must conform with the sense of the citation.

> ... we feel the need constantly to examine techniques and routines to insure the best service.³

This way, in confronting the department as a user, the serials manager gets the best picture of the system's real worth. And in this, it provides the best stimulus for re-examination and appropriate improvement.

Physical Location of Serials

The one aspect of the serials system yet to be addressed is the problem of physical location. A suggested arrangement is to have the serials staff situated directly adjacent to, or within, the stacks themselves. However, the usual necessary clutter associated with the unwrapping and checking-in procedures is a strong disadvantage here, especially if the collection is an open one. What such an arrangement does achieve, however, is a re-definition of the reference service. Instead of being an extension of the reference desk, the serials staff are now the principal reference point for all serials queries. Unfortunately, an addition disadvantage of this arrangement is the administrative problems of staffing yet another public point during off-hours.

This question of open versus closed stacks, then, has a number of implications. The re-defining of the reference activity means a significantly reduced burden for the "general" reference staff, and may instead create a kind of "serials reference" unit. In closed-stack situations, where the contact desk is staffed exclusively by serials people, it is true that some tighter control results from having no "outsiders" handling and interpreting the records. But again, this is often administratively inadvisable, since so much additional staff is required for all these things, over and above all the routines of documentation.

The stack arrangement also partly determines the location of records. If the stacks are entirely open and unstaffed, it is strongly advisable to have public holdings records available nearby. But closed stacks eliminate the need for this duplication. Here is perhaps where automation makes its most profound contribution to serials. Additional terminals or printouts can accompany the collection wherever it is housed. Automation, then, does not speed up the documenting procedures, as much as it makes them both more universally known and more reliably interpreted.

It would seem, then, that the most feasible arrangement is the middle ground where the serials and reference departments must consistently interact with each other. It is most sensible to leave the principal reference aspects of serials to the reference staff, made possible by an efficient and professional serials staff in providing the accurate and reliable documentation.

Serials, in all their mysterious varieties, are in many ways the library's most fascinating element, increasing in prominence as they multiply in numbers. And with this universally-growing importance, one thing is certain — the interplay between technical mechanism and public delivery has never before held such status.

NOTES

1. Donald Davinson, *The Periodicals Collection*, revised and enlarged edition. (Boulder: Westview Press, 1978), p. 191.

2. Elaine Walker, "Serials in a College Library," *Library Resources & Technical Services* 6 (1962), 81.

3. Edith Clitheroe, "Serials in a University Library," *Library Resources & Technical Services* 6 (1962), 92.

SERIALS:
SEPARATE OR MERGED?

Jennifer Cargill

The establishment of technical service and public service divisions became a major trend in libraries in the 1940s. Serials departments were often among those separate departments created within the new division structure. Between 1950 and the mid-1970s serials gained a strong identity within technical services. Increasingly, serials was viewed as a unique and separate function and the recording of serials was considered to be a highly specialized task.

In 1976, Dunlap was urging libraries to "develop systems which make the most efficient use of all resources and to correct organizational patterns which result in expensive or inadequate service."[1] In 1979, Gorman was challenging his colleagues with such statements as: "The present economic situation forces us to use our human and technical resources as efficiently as possible."[2]

In the 1980s, there is an increasing amount of emphasis on performance, especially on doing work in an efficient and cost effective manner. This emphasis has required organizations to be flexible enough to make the necessary adjustments. And, as a result, there is now a clear trend in many libraries to eliminate separate serials departments and to merge personnel and duties into other departments.

Is there a justification to make such drastic changes in the traditional organizational structure? Will those changes create problems? What about the careers of those people who have been trained to be serials librarians? And finally, will such an organizational change produce significant benefits for the library?

Common Characteristics

Behind the abolition of the separate serials departments is a movement toward dividing up existing work according to function rather than form. Merging monograph acquisitions and serials acquisitions into a single department has been the natural result in many instances. At the acquisitions stage, there is considerable similarity between books and serials. With serials collections in a rather stable state, with relatively few new subscriptions being added and more concern being voiced for the identification of titles to cancel, there has been a general feeling expressed that serials operations could be effectively merged into other departments. Where such mergers are occurring, serials departments are being absorbed along functional lines. In these merged departments, the same group of people process all the acquisitions of materials and a similar group handles the cataloging.

The structure of the newly merged departments varies from situations in which everyone does some of the work to instances in which some individuals remain performing specialized routines within the combined department. Is there enough similarity of routines to warrant an efficient combination of book and serial functions? For both functions:

- ——Bibliographic information must be verified and library holdings, if any, established.
- ——Materials must be ordered from a vendor who may be a wholesaler, publisher, or a subscription agency.
- ——Follow-up work may be necessary if the items ordered are not received in due course.
- ——All materials must be officially received and noted properly in the records. Mystery items must be investigated.
- ——Invoices must be approved for prompt payment.
- ——The received materials must be forwarded to the user or to the next processing stage on a regular schedule.

Within monograph acquisitions, there may be a great deal of preliminary work necessary prior to placing the order including the bibliographic searching and verification of either the bibliographic record itself or the order information. Once the book is received, there may be additional checking of the received items against the original order to be certain that what was ordered is indeed what has been received. However, acquisitions' interest in the item ceases once that item is officially received and sent on to the next stage of processing, usually the catalog department, and when the invoices have been paid. Thus, with books, there may be much preparation activity up until the item is sent on to cataloging, but at that point Acquisitions interest in the item ceases.

With serials, there is considerable bibliographic searching prior to placing the order. Once the items have been ordered, they will be received regularly (or irregularly) but definitely on a periodic and continuing basis. This is true of both continuations and periodicals.

Once the subscription begins, processing activity becomes a matter of receiving the item, making sure the subscriptions are paid on a regular basis, or in the case of monographic serials, are paid upon receipt of the volume. Processing of current issues or numbers is the most demanding, ongoing phase of serials activity. The check-in staff must be adequate in numbers and in their skills to make certain that check-in activity doesn't fall behind. In addition to the recording function, the check-in unit also confirms receipt and provides necessary data prior to renewing subscriptions and making payments.

The Differences

The *additional* factor that has contributed greatly to the mystique of serials, as opposed to book acquisitions, has been that periodicals and series change titles on an all too regular basis — and that these title changes must be correctly identified and noted on all processing and cataloging records. In addition, format and issuing periods change with serials in a way that is not characteristic of monograph acquisitions. These differences in behavior and bibliographic information have probably done more to create the unique quality of serials work than any other single factor.

However, once an order or subscription is established for a serial (and assuming there are no problems with the vendor or publisher supplying the materials) there should be little additional work to be accomplished beyond keeping track of the changes. Title and format changes can usually be caught at the time the item is received *if* the staff has been properly trained to be alert to such changes. In addition, all the major subscription agencies now provide updating services that automatically alert the library whenever changes occur.

Relatively little bibliographic work is now required: the bibliographic work that *is* needed involves only a relatively few troublesome titles rather than all the items being acquired. Thus, with a subscription base of 5,000 titles that was established many years ago, a very small percentage of the titles will actually need additional searching or verification. At the same time, in any given year, that same library may be acquiring 20,000–30,000 new book titles, all of which require extensive bibliographic work. Few libraries are continuing to set up large numbers of new subscriptions or serials orders. Those that are can usually rely on the bibliographic utilities to supply much of the verification work while their subscription agencies supply additional information about title or format changes or ongoing problems with the subscriptions.

But what about the problems that arise upon from unfilled periodical subscriptions or standing orders? A serials librarian's approach to solving such a problem should be very much the same as a monographic acquisitions librarian's approach. Indeed, the job qualifications for serials librarians are generally the same as those for acquisitions librarians. And since these problem-solving routines should be similar why can't the same people, that is the same staff, deal with those problems? Just as the book acquisitions librarian must stay on top of problems whether they be claims, incorrect shipments, or invoice problems, the serials librarian, if he/she is an effective manager must remain similarly alert.

Certain kinds of routine claiming may be more of a problem within the area of serials than they are with books. A single book order may be claimed one or two or three times but a serials subscription may be claimed dozens and dozens of times over several years. Of course, having a definite procedure for reviewing the check-in records and staying up-to-date on the claims will make this such a routine part of the day-to-day operation that is will not become a burden.

Personnel Performance

One unfortunate by-product of the technical services and public services organizational pattern was the creation of stereotypes for technical services librarians that were far more severe and damaging than that of librarians in general. Catalogers and serials librarians and to some extent acquisitions librarians, contributed to their image within the library world by encouraging and even fostering a belief that their work is highly complex, even unique. The cataloging is so complex, specialized, and intricate or that serials are so completely different from every other type of materials acquired in libraries and working with serials is very special are examples of many beliefs encouraged over the years. Some catalog and serials departments have lead us to believe that they perform highly specialized work, requiring librarians with special talents who can treat the work in a very precise way. Some acquisitions librarians have generated the same image by becoming "super searchers" employing needlessly complex search routines and demanding large staffs while still accumulating a backlog of unsearched and unfilled requests.

When merging the two departments, these stereotypes will tend to disappear. There simply won't be enough time available to perpetuate the image. Routine processing of serial and book materials should require little or no professional involvement.

Most of these functions do not require the expertise of librarians. Technicians will be better utilized for accessing data bases so an extensive knowledge of the literature and traditional tools will be less important. Split assignments between the book and serial units of acquisitions will also result in better staff understanding of the importance of their jobs in the entire organization as well as an improved comprehension of the importance of other people's jobs. It will also remove the mystery of the respective operations. One of the biggest pitfalls in contemplating such a merger will involve the staff. You may find yourself with an entrenched serials librarian who will not want to give up the prestige of separate departmental status. He/she will emphasize the minutiae and the specialized nature of the work. *Or*, you may have an entrenched acquisitions librarian who similarly does not want to give up the prestige of separate departmental status. Either the serials or acquisitions librarian may claim no knowledge of the other area and be reluctant to take on any additional duties. One or the other will be the stronger, more effective manager – or a third person may be or even an outsider – and the better manager should be given the task of merging the two departments. How you handle the new department name, select the manager and establish the image you want the department to project are all important considerations. The attitude of the people involved (supervisors, workers, and department head) will be all important to the success of the merger. They must have a positive "can do" attitude.

When merging these two departments, it is vital to select a manager who is willing to deal with the issues as they arise. He/she must stay on top of activities and work hard to devise procedures to eliminate unnecessary work. Reviewing the services available from a book or serials vendor may lead the manager to discover that certain services they can provide will save days or week or time within the acquisitions department. Use of such services may allow internal streamlining of work to the extent that other duties may be assigned to those staff members who have been freed from very tedious routines.

Successful Merger

The very best justification for such merger is improved performance of the resulting organization. But before contemplating such a change, find out exactly what the current procedures are and examine them carefully. Discuss the proposed changes with the existing staff; they may be the best source for discovering time wasting, unnecessary procedures that can be eliminated. Point out the advantages of the flexibility that will result from cross training. Coordinating the total acquisitions functions, eliminating overlap areas, and producing a better trained staff for all phases of acquisitions work will ensure that the new department will be better able to do its part in the library's service mission.

The book-oriented unit of the department may have inherited a negative attitude toward serials. They are accustomed to a sense of accomplishment in the one-time processing that is characteristic of their work. Serials are ongoing and not always very straightforward.

Attitudes that have been built up over a long time will be hard to change.

As the staff sees the advantages of cross-training, they will see that shifts in staff duties are possible. Merging may also increase the productivity of the new department. When one unit is low on work its staff can be assigned to help another unit. When that unit runs into problems and is having difficulty keeping up, the other unit can help. Staff can be cross trained very effectively to provide back up for all assignments. Projects can be pre-planned to be handled as staff has time. Priorities can be identified and established. Combining the work and improving productivity will mean that as employee turnover occurs, you may be able to leave a position unfilled, merge responsibilities, or even transfer unused salaries into the books and periodicals budget. Under utilized staff can continue to work on special ongoing projects or even be transferred to other departments where they can be utilized more effectively.

Administration and the librarians involved should take a very hard look at what work is performed in the purchase of materials and then start questioning long standing traditions and consider merging similar functions so that materials are ordered and received, whether it is a one-time receipt or an ongoing commitment.

NOTES

1. Dunlap, Connie R. "Organizational Patterns in Academic Libraries, 1876–1976." *College and Research Libraries*, 37 (1976), 396.

2. Gorman, Michael. "On Doing Away with Technical Services." *American Libraries*, 10 (1979), 435.

BACKGROUND READING

Bartley, Linda K. "Serials Section Medium-Sized Research Libraries Discussion Group." *LC Information Bulletin*. 39 (1980) 345–346.
    Discussion group discussed abolition of serial departments.

Brown, Clara, D. and Lynn S. Smith. *Serials: Past, Present and Future*. 2d (rev.) edition. Birmingham: EBSCO, 1980: 20–22.
    Book covers all aspects of serials but these pages include discussion of organization of serials departments.

Burgis, G.C. "A Systems Concept of Organization and Control for Large University Libraries." *Canadian Library*, 28 (1971), 24–29.
    A Canadian view that traditional structure in large university libraries is on verge of collapse, that is in 1971.

Dunlap, Connie R. "Organizational Patterns in Academic Libraries, 1876–1976." *College and Research Libraries*, 37 (1976), 395–407.
    Organization of library should make effective use of resources. Changes in organizational patterns over a century.

Dyal, Donald H. "A Survey of Serials Management in Texas." *Texas Libraries*, 38 (1976), 164–172.
    Organizational structure of serials departments in Texas is based on historical factors.

Ford, Stephen. *The Acquisition of Library Materials*. Rev. ed. Chicago: ALA, 1978: 24–25.
    Ford found most common organization is to assign acquisitions and recording of serials to acquisitions and cataloging of serials to catalog department.

Gapen, D. Kaye and Ichicko T. Moreta. "OCLC at OSU: The Effect of the Adoption of OCLC on the Management of Technical Services at a Large Academic Library. *Library Resources and Technical Services*, 22 (1978), 5–21.
    The evolution of several different organizational structures at OSU over a period of serveral years during the 1970s.

Gorman, Michael. "On Doing Away with Technical Services Departments." *American Libraries*, 10 (1979), 435–437.
    Free professionals from non-professional activities and "use human and technical resources as efficiently as possible."

Kennedy, Gail. "Technical Processing Librarians in the 1980's: Current Trends and Future Forecasts." *University of Kentucky Libraries Occasional Papers*, 1 (August 1980).
    Discussion of the many possible and probable changes in technical services as automation increases and buying power decreases.

Lang, Jovian P. "Serials Management." *The Catholic Library World*, 47 (1976), 401–402.
    Will we see the demise of serials as we know them?

Melin, Nancy Jean. "The Public Service Functions of Serials." *Serials Review*, 6:1 (1980), 39–44.
   Different patterns of organization and use for serials.

Osborn, Andrew D. *Serial Publications; Their Place and Treatment in Libraries*. 3d ed. Chicago: ALA, 1980: 57–72.
   Chapter is on organization of serial work and where it falls in library structure.

Tuttle, Helen W. "From Cutter to Computer: Technical Service in Academic and Research Libraries, 1876–1976," 37 (1976), 421–451.
   From 1950–1975 serials identity within technical services became stronger.

Weber, Benita M. "Education of Serials Librarians: A Survey." *Drexel Library Quarterly*, 11 (1975), 72–81.
   Library schools do not provide adequate training for serials librarians.

Weber, Hans H. "Serials Administration." *Serials Librarian*, 4 (1979), 143–165.
   Proper administration of serials is very important to libraries. A discussion of different organization structures, personnel, etc.

THE ROLE OF THE CENTRAL SERIALS UNIT
IN AN AUTOMATED LIBRARY

Mitsuko Collver

In view of the trend toward increasing applications of computer technology to library operations, especially in the technical services, some librarians have begun to consider the consequences of the new technology for the organization of library activities and personnel. Indeed this is an opportune time to review and re-evaluate the organization of libraries in general and of technical services in particular. Since the computer is causing a revolution in many other aspects of library services it seems reasonable to expect that it could revolutionize library organization as well.

At the same time, we should bear in mind that technology need not be the only criterion by which organizational alternatives are judged. The enormous capabilities of the computer may not limit us to only one best way of organizing, but instead may allow a variety of options from among which we may still be able to choose according to standards of cost-effectiveness, productivity and quality of service. Certainly the earlier technology of typewriters, 3 x 5 cards, duplicating machines and Kardex files allowed a wide range of administrative structures, and it could be argued that automation will be more of a liberating than a constraining influence.

The primary role of a serials unit regardless of its configuration is service to the library's users. The final products of the serials activities in a given library are serials publications in all forms processed and shelved for the patrons' use, and manual or on-line catalogs and holdings information pertaining to these materials.

In order to provide these services, libraries carry out several activities on-line or off-line which will be referred to here as "serials operations." These include, under the general heading of *acquisitions*, preorder searching, ordering, paying, maintaining the central serials record, receiving and checking-in, claiming, delivery of issues to the shelves, and binding. Under *cataloging* the operations are bibliographic decisions and control, precatalog searching, cataloging, recataloging, series decisions and producing and maintaining the catalog. *Public services* include maintaining the public serials file or list, updating holdings information, and servicing periodicals in the reading room or by telephone.

Organization for Coordination

The basic issue with regard to serials organization has to do with the grouping of these operations for coordination. Existing practices in various libraries include assigning some of the operations to the cataloging department and others to the acquisitions department or establishing a separate serials department that performs all or some of the operations while other functions remain with cataloging and acquisitions. With the growth of computer-assisted operations still other solutions are being mentioned, including the creation of a super-unit for technical processing for acquisitions, cataloging and serials, but with check-in of issues for branch libraries performed at the branches and with cataloging assigned to subject specialists in the public service areas of the library.[1] The latter proposal contains two opposite tendencies: one is to centralize technical services to a much higher degree than before, but the other is to decentralize by assigning some of the serials operations to public service units.

Chronic financial problems as well as automation seem to be the major forces leading some libraries to come up with new ideas for the organization of technical processing. A number of organizational and procedural changes were involved in at least one library as it adopted the OCLC system.[1] Disappearance of serials units as distinct entities in some major libraries has been reported.[2] Gorman argues that the pressures of automation, financial constraints and the search for professionalism in librarianship will shape a new kind of library in which a centralized automated processing operation is staffed primarily by nonprofessionals while professional librarians are grouped around special subjects and services.[3] Lancaster and others (1980) forecast that local technical services in general will dwindle away since libraries will be acquiring much less material within the next decade or so.[4] The on-line text will become widely accessible, printed subscriptions will be cancelled, and interlibrary loan activities will be reduced.

In weighing the pros and cons of the different organizational designs that have been proposed, we should bear in mind that the serials processing system in a library includes three major groups of factors. These are technology, organization and personnel. All of these factors are interdependent and should be designed to be compatible. However, none of them fully determines the others. With a given form of technology, a variety of alternate forms of organizations are possible. The choice among these forms cannot be made on the basis of the technology, but has to be made on other grounds.

Likewise, once the technology and organization are in place a variety of different styles and policies of personnel involvement are inconceivable, and the choice among them should be made on grounds of human needs and motivations as these can be related to the goals of the library.

Automation and Organization

There can be no disputing the fact that automation of libraries has consequences for their forms of organization. Before going into the subject of organizational design, we should be clear about the nature of these effects. Three types of effects will be considered here. The first is the impact on the composition of technical services units in terms of the number of personnel, the division of labor, and the type, quantity and location of facilities and equipment. Automation also affects the structure of technical services by changing the degree and types of interdependence between operations. It thus emphatically affects their need for coordination. Finally, automation has far-reaching impacts on interunit relations between the various technical services (e.g., between the acquisitions unit and the cataloging unit), between the technical services and public services departments, and also between the library and book dealers. Virtually synonymous with automation is a vast increase in the scale of interlibrary information networks and regional resource sharing.

By use of a central data base via terminals, beginning with on-line shared cataloging, library technical services have been successful in achieving speed and cost effectiveness. Most medium and large libraries are in a transitional stage in their use of automation. Today many of them are capable of searching, cataloging and producing catalog cards on-line via terminals. Conversion from card catalogs to on-line catalogs, if not done yet, will be the next step. On-line check-in of serials, claiming, binding, union lists and ordering are being planned or are in process of conversion. Many major subscription vendors have automated their operations and libraries are benefiting from better service as well as from the use of various printouts that are valuable in budget control and collection development work. Some vendors have begun to offer on-line acquisitions packages of their own, an activity which parallels the major networks' efforts to develop acquisitions systems.

Conversion from manual to complete on-line systems will take many years. During the transitional period the workload remains high as personnel are required to maintain the manual system, to carry out projects of conversion to on-line systems, and to operate the new systems.

Meanwhile, early imperfections in the cooperative data base

continue to make extra work for technical services staff. Many libraries, for example, find it necessary to verify and improve OCLC member records before adopting them (Braden, 1980).[5]

In libraries where the new technology has been applied to various degrees, typists whose efforts are no longer needed to type catalog cards now work at terminals converting retrospective bibliographic records. Increasingly, paraprofessionals and clerical staff are involved in on-line cataloging where little or no modification of records is required. Only original cataloging and extensive cataloging revisions are given to the serials catalogers. Similar impacts on personnel assignments will be felt when a serials control subsystem is introduced for the operations of checking-in, claiming and control of binding.

Automation and Library Organization

With this brief sketch of the progress of library automation, we can begin to discuss its potential effects on library organization. The change in the nature of the objects worked on — from paper records to electronic data bases, and eventually from books in hard copy to text on-line — at first may call for an increase in staffing requirements. This is true since during the transition both the old and the new systems must be in simultaneous operation and in addition conversion projects call for additional staff time. Once the transition has been made, however, automation eliminates much of the need for clerical staff to type, produce, and file cards. Eventually it should also allow for a reduction of the staff needed for such tasks as opening mail, checking-in, shelving, binding and updating holdings of serial records. Cataloging tasks are also reduced locally as more cataloging is shared nationally. The reduction in number of personnel increases the feasibility of combining the various technical services into one super-unit.

The cutback in original cataloging, nevertheless, will not do away with the need for professional librarians who maintain bibliographic control of the library's unique local collection, catalog archival materials, and serve as problem solvers for library staff and patrons lost in the maze of serials problems.

The spread of access terminals to different parts of the library, to branch libraries, to academic offices and eventually to the homes of faculty may at first appear to make decentralization of technical services more feasible. However, on close scrutiny we can see that it is output to users that is being decentralized. Input is quite another matter, for it requires central coordination and supervision for quality control, completeness and timeliness of entries.

Automated serials control will present the necessity for a clear organizational choice. In many institutions, serials are checked-in and processed centrally and then sent to branch or departmental libraries where they are again checked-in. Automation will obviate the need for more than a single check-in. A decision will have to be made as to whether it is to be done centrally or in the branches.

Automation reduces the cost of sharing such resources as the shelf list, authority file and cataloging tools among the various technical services operations. In this respect, it favors decentralization of technical services by weakening the argument that, for example, serials catalogers and monographs catalogers should be grouped together to share the shelf list.

On the interlibrary level of organization, the new technology coupled with the growing volume and cost of publications, exerts a compelling influence for large scale cooperative networks. On the local level, however, it appears to have more of a diversifying influence. At this level, automation opens up more possibilities for organization than the simpler technologies. Instead of settling the question of serials organization, automation leaves us with more choices than before.

The Central Serials Unit

If the foregoing analysis is correct, the new technology raises the prospect of even more diversity among libraries of the future than we have seen in the recent past. My view, as presented in an earlier essay is that such diversity is not a healthy sign of adaptation to differing local needs, but, instead, a symptom of the failure to develop a sound rationale for organization.[6] Perhaps we need a "science of serials" that will enable us to develop guidelines for more effective organization.

As a step toward a more systematic approach to serials management, I have recommended a set of principles of coordination that were formulated by Thompson.[7] When two activities are interdependent, coordination is required so that they will affect one another in a mutually beneficial way.

According to Thompson, there are three kinds of interdependence, each having its own coordination requirements. The simplest type, *pooled* interdependence arises by use of a common resource or facilities. Coordination of the use of a common resource is relatively easy and inexpensive to accomplish through standardization and rules. As a result there is little need for grouping the activities together.

The second type is *sequential* interdependence. In this type there is a one way flow of operations in the manner of an assembly line. Sequential interdependence is coordinated by plans and scheduling. The cost of coordination and the necessity for grouping activities together are higher in case of sequential interdependence than in pooled interdependence.

In the most complex type of interdependence, *reciprocal*, each function requires repeated inputs from and interaction with the other functions. The work process cannot be predetermined by plans but must be carried out by mutual adjustment between the workers and the object they are working on. This type of interdependence presents the highest costs of coordination, and the greatest necessity for grouping activities together.

Reciprocal Interdependence of Serials

In library work, the serials operations of preorder searching, ordering, paying, receiving and checking-in, claiming, updating holdings information, precatalog searching, cataloging, recataloging, production and maintenance of the catalog, binding, and public service of periodicals are reciprocally interdependent. None of the major operations can continue for long without calling at least some of the others into play. Even the simple act of checking-in a monthly issue can set off a round of interactions throughout the serials processing system in response to information contained on the cover of the issue. Every time the title or issuing body changes, the publisher or frequency changes, the publication is suspended, ceases, or resumes, the size or format changes, special issues appear, or subscription and standing orders are cancelled or added, the routine flow of processing is interrupted. It cannot be continued until information and decisions are received from others. For this reason, all serials related activities should be grouped into one unit for the benefit of maximum coordination. Serials management consists of supervision and coordination of these serials activities. Management can be effective only when the functions are grouped and organized in a way that will both facilitate communication among them and also assure that decisions affecting any one function will support the other functions.

It is essential that serials catalogers be included in the central serials unit because bibliographic decision making is the controlling activity for all the other serials activities. Serials catalogers possess the knowledge required for this work, and their intimate participation and assistance are essential to maintain a high quality of service.

Public service is also an integral part of serials operations. While serials personnel are not equipped to deal with general reference questions, which properly belong in the reference department, they are in the best position to answer questions about the location and availability of current issues. The current periodicals reading room is the interface between the public and the technical services, and it is best served by the personnel of the central serials unit. Current unbound and incomplete volumes are still in technical processing, even though they are shelved in the public area for patrons' use. Serials personnel coordinate delivery, shelving, removing for binding and retention decisions, and searching for missing issues and indexes. Some issues are to be replaced by microforms or prebound volumes or to be cataloged or discarded. All of these functions are performed by the central serials unit. Some unbound volumes with special problems are often temporarily housed in the serials office but should be accessible to the patrons when wanted.

Problem Solving Benefits

By gathering all the reciprocally interdependent serials activities and personnel together in one unit it is possible to improve many of the shortcomings and solve problems relating to serials operations. First of all, communication can be improved among serials related workers, and physical fragmentation of serials work, files and personnel can be eliminated.

The central serials unit can develop a flexible pool of manpower, talent and specialized technical knowledge. Personnel can be cross trained to be able to meet temporary assignments to assist in different areas of serials activities in the event of sudden personnel shortages due to illness, vacation, hiring freeze or personnel cutbacks, so that there will be no interruption in the basic daily operations of receiving and checking-in. Seasonal peaks of demand at the public service counter again call for ability to shift personnel from one task to another. The required flexibility of manpower can only be attained in a fairly large group of workers who share a common core of knowledge and experience. The availability of a wide variety of talent and knowledge are advantageous in serials work. For example, special drawers for Russian, Oriental and other difficult languages can be set up in the Kardex and the language experts regardless of their rank and major responsibilities in the serials unit can check them in quickly and accurately.

In the central serials unit the various projects of conversion from manual to on-line systems, which nowadays are ongoing programs in many research libraries, can be accomplished efficiently and smoothly. Conversion requires coordination, setting of priorities, and communication among various serials functions. When the functions are grouped in one unit for coordination the application of the new technology can be accomplished with the least friction and delay.

The final advantage to be cited for the central serials unit is that it establishes responsibility and accountability for serials work. In medium and large libraries there must be someone on a full-time basis who is responsible for the coordination of all serials activities. This person should also be in a position to advocate the interests of the unit throughout the library and to obtain resources and policies in support of its mission.

In the central serials unit, formed to minimize the costs of co-ordination of reciprocally interdependent activities, the library's task of providing access to serial publications can be effectively and efficiently achieved. When serials operations are brought together in one unit. greater productivity and a higher degree of quality control will be obtained than in any other administrative arrangement of serials activities.

The Human Factor

Every bit as important as designing an efficient production system is the necessity for creating a supportive and cooperative environment for people. As long as serials operations require people, and not just machines and computers, human relations and human feelings have an important role in the overall accomplishment of the unit's mission.

In the Library of the State University of New York at Stony Brook, where the ideas presented here were developed, implemented and evaluated, most of the former problems in serials handling were traceable to organizational factors. These factors in turn had led to a number of problems in the area of human motivation. The most basic of these was that personnel were scattered in different departments and sections performing parts of the serials operations but never having the opportunity to see the whole or to understand the overall public service mission. The result, of course, was a classic case of worker alienation from the products of their labor.

In the new Serials Department, which was organized in 1975, special efforts were made to break down the mental barriers that had developed between the various serials sections in the library. The aim was to develop a sense of belonging, loyalty and commitment to the Serials Department and its goals. Training sessions were held on the overall operations and products of the department, and members were given opportunities to become involved in different tasks according to their ability and wishes. Cross training and participation by staff in a variety of special projects outside of their normal routine converted an aggregation of narrow specialists into a team of versatile and cooperative workers who were ready to help one another as needed to achieve collective goals.

Especially valuable in overcoming alienation was the practice of assigning everyone to take turns at the current periodicals counter.

Serials receivers who are assigned daily to serve the counter for a brief period of time by taking turns not only enjoy a break from receiving and claiming but gain at first hand a sense of the urgency and importance of their daily tasks. It also gives them a feeling of reward and pleasure when they can assist the patrons satisfactorily. Otherwise the technical services personnel would have very little opportunity to enjoy the satisfaction of serving patrons. Also at the same time they experience and observe the patrons' disappointment when an issue is missing due to the receivers' tardiness in claiming.

The human implications of grouping serials staff together as a unit were well understood and aptly expressed by Weber. He notes "a strong negative psychological attitude toward serials in major units that are primarily book-oriented." This attitude creates a tendency to put serials aside "in hopes that they will go away if ignored."[8] In the integrated serials unit, in contrast, staff become familiar with the vagaries of "this complicated genre," and come to look upon their work with pride. "Such an attitude goes far toward a much more efficient processing work flow and a substantial decrease in a natural reluctance to put aside an unfamiliar form that 'outsiders' usually associate with nothing but unpleasant problems."

Pride of workmanship, willingness to grapple with a problem until it is solved, and an interest in prompt delivery of materials to the shelves as well as accurate and prompt recording and filing of bibliographic and receipt data — these are psychological factors, and yet they are intricately related to the structure of serials organization. A fragmented serials processing system discourages efforts to solve those unpleasant problems because the needed resources, information and advice are too scattered and too well hidden behind departmental walls to be usefully available. Staff in the unified serials organization develop a "can do" attitude because in fact they have at their command the tools with which to succeed.

Conclusions

The main line of the preceding argument and the conclusions drawn may be summed up with the following eight points.
1. Technology alone cannot solve the problems of serials handling. An effective structure for coordination and for bringing out the human potential of the personnel is also necessary.
2. Automation tends to widen the range of possible forms of organization of serials operations rather than to restrict it.
3. Automation with terminals in scattered locations reduces the need for grouping together of users of the output from the data base; it does not, however, reduce the need for coordination of the input of records into the file. Data input

operations remain reciprocally interdependent and can work most productively when grouped together.
4. The central serials unit, grouping together the reciprocally interdependent serials operations, remains as effective with automation as with manual systems.
5. The dependence of all other operations upon bibliographic control places the serials cataloger in a key coordinating role that is essential to the functioning of the central serials unit.
6. Once an on-line serials control system is operational, local data records will be accessible from different locations. This will eliminate the need for duplicate check-in for branch libraries. Since check-in involves input to the on-line file, it is most appropriately assigned to the central unit.
7. The central serials unit is entirely compatible with, and indeed facilitates, the acceptance of automation.
8. Because of their complexity, serials especially require the full attention and top priority efforts of well trained personnel who are dedicated to the goals of serials management. The central serials unit provides the required focus and incentive structure.

For the foreseeable future until "electronic" or "paperless" libraries arrive, the handling of serials will continue to require mutual adjustment and reciprocal interaction among the several operations. Coordination of these activities is best obtained in a central serials unit combining all serials related operations of cataloging, acquisitions and public service of current periodicals. With serials catalogers responsible for bibliographic control, and with a librarian in charge of overall management, this unit has the capability of maintaining current work flow even while it is in the process of adopting new technology. At the same time it serves as a supportive environment in which staff development and participation can be fostered.

NOTES

1. Kaye D. Gapen and Ichiko T. Morita. "OCLC at OSU: The Effect of the Adoption of OCLC on the Management of Technical Services at a Large Academic Library." *Library Resources & Technical Services* 22 (1978), 5–21.

2. Peter Gellatly. "Deserialization." *The Serials Librarian* 4 (1980), 367–369.

3. Michael Gorman. "On Doing Away with Technical Services Departments." *American Libraries* 10 (1979), 435–437.

4. Wilfrid F. Lancaster, Laura S. Drasgow and Ellen B. Marks. "The Role of the Library in an Electronic Society." In F. Wilfrid Lancaster, ed., *Proceedings of the 1979 Clinic on Library Applications of Data Processing: The Role of the Library in an Electronic Society*. Urbana, IL: University of Illinois, Graduate School of Library Science, 1980: 162–189.

5. Sally Braden, John D. Hall and Helen H. Britton. "Utilization of Personnel and Bibliographic Resources for Cataloging by OCLC Participating Libraries." *Library Resources & Technical Services* 24 (1980), 135–154.

6. Mitsuko Collver. "Organization of Serials Work for Manual and Automated Systems." *Library Resources & Technical Services* 24 (1980), 307–316.

7. James D. Thompson. *Organizations in Action*. New York: Mc Graw-Hill, 1967.

8. Hans H. Weber. "Serials Administration." *Serials Librarian* 4 (1979), 143–165.

?. "Technical Services in an Automated Library," in F. Wilfrid Lancaster, ed., *Proceedings of the 1979 Clinic on Library Applications of Data Processing: The Role of the Library in an Electronic Society*. Urbana, IL: University of Illinois, Graduate School of Library Science, 1980: 48–59.

SERIALS STAFFING GUIDELINES FOR THE 80'S

Margaret McKinley

The halcyon decade of the sixties is far behind us and the gray, grim eighties stretch endlessly before us. Those serials specialists whose departments have been dismembered cry out that there is no opportunity to practice the craft of serials management. Those who are struggling with inadequate book budgets, insufficient staff or unsympathetic library administrators complain that they cannot stretch book dollars any further and cannot ask their staffs to assume additional tasks. Are we then to concede defeat and retire whimpering to our offices in meek anticipation of the inevitable collapse all around us of mountains of unbound periodicals and stacks of delinquent invoices?

How is a serials manager to organize a serials department or unit to meet the challenges of a rapidly changing world in which technological, economic or political developments occur so rapidly that we scarcely can create a nomenclature for one phenomenon before the next one is upon us? Is the future bleak for the continued vigor of serials collection management in libraries? Surely not, if obstacles can be regarded as challenges on which to test the limits of the ingenuity and inventiveness lying dormant in the imaginations of serials specialists and waiting for discovery.

Modification of the serials manager's own perspective on serials management could provide renewed energy and creativity. Transformation of a basic management approach, in today's rapidly changing library environment, must begin with the admission that no organization is perfect and that perfection may well be unattainable. A staffing pattern and workflow which is ideal in one set of circumstances may well have disastrous consequences in another. Serials managers strive for perfection, recognizing that even as they struggle the external world is changing, forcing them to alter staffing structures, job assignments, materials flow and processing plans. For instance, as a library that is card-oriented and has a handsome book budget gradually metamorphoses into one which is terminal-oriented and has a meager book budget, its administrators and managers must alter the library's organization, procedures and communication patterns in order to master changing environmental conditions.

Having conceded that imperfection in an organization is inevitable, serials specialists must then recognize that the only sensible solution is to organize for change, to anticipate it and to plan for it. This is scarcely a new concept and has its roots in that well-worn aphorism, "If you can't beat 'em, join 'em." In order to maintain a smoothing functioning unit, a serials manager must encourage the development of a staff that is capable of meeting any challenge in the present and whose forces can be redeployed to handle the crises of the week or month.

The third important step in altering one's management perspective is to identify the nature and scope of the problems to be solved as well as the obstacles to be overcome. In order to manage collections and staff efficiently, serials specialists must learn to identify emerging trends and to anticipate changes in library or institutional policies and practices. The challenges facing serials managers at this time appear to have their roots in two major areas: those related to the economy (inflation, rising wages, static or declining budgets, and lack of funds for capital improvements) and those related to technology or, more specifically, automation and its consequences (file conversion, dual processing systems, staff retraining and reorganization).

While these issues can be set out neatly for purposes of discussion, they do interact with one another in a complex fashion. For example, some library administrators look upon automation of processing activities in libraries as a significant means of reducing the effect of rising wages on labor-intensive operations. In libraries headed by these individuals, it may be difficult to obtain funds to hire a bibliographic checker but money is readily available to develop or to implement a computer-assisted processing system.

Creation and maintenance of an effective and efficient staff in a serials unit is crucial to successful resolution of economic and technological challenges. Close attention to certain aspects of management will assist a serials manager in the development of such a staff. These aspects are communication and leadership, deployment of professionals and nonprofessionals, and recruiting and retaining staff. If a serials manager makes appropriate plans well in advance, the effects of possible budgetary reverses may be greatly reduced. Automation, the optimists' great hope and the pessimists' great fear, depends heavily for its success on an enthusiastic staff, carefully prepared for the radical changes which automation brings in its wake.

Communication and Leadership

Reitz noted in *Behavior in Organizations* that, if tasks to be accomplished were complex, decentralized communication networks produced performance superior to centralized networks. The efficiency of centralized networks broke down because of the amount of information and communication that a single individual, at the center of the network, was required to handle. If tasks are complex, groups using centralized communication networks make more errors and reach solutions more slowly than groups using decentralized networks.[1]

The implications for serials managers of these research findings are clear. Serials workers are usually engaged in complex tasks. They are energetic and talented individuals who ought to be given as much autonomy and freedom to innovate as possible. The serials unit manager who encourages supervisors to work with one another in resolution of problems will be able to take credit for a more smoothly functioning department. Delegation of decision-making responsibility may reduce employee attrition. In addition, it frees the serials unit manager for activities beyond the daily monitoring and supervision of routine processing or public services tasks. Most importantly, however, the unit manager has the assistance of many more flexible and innovative minds bearing down on the problems of the day.

An integral part of the complexity of serials processing or of providing access to serials publications is the frequency with which processes, procedures, information and materials must cross the artificial boundaries of a library's organizational structure. A serials unit's efficiency will be enhanced if workers feel free to cross organizational boundaries without the specific knowledge or permission of the unit manager. If the serials staff is encouraged to work with one another and to discuss mutual concerns across subunits or with other library units the objectives of the unit will be met more readily. Discussions or conferences with staff in other library units or departments and with serials vendors should not only be approved by the serials manager but should be actively promoted.

The most difficult task for many serials managers is to permit the staff of a serials unit to develop its own methods of handling problems, to break with a library's traditions and to try new methods which may, or may not, be successful. While encouraging the serials unit's staff to work independently, many serials managers may wish to recommend that their supervisors keep them informed of any dramatic changes planned so that the manager can provide appropriate support.

A word of caution must be inserted here. A serials manager, whose previous practice has been to discourage independent conferences or consultations among a unit's staff or with staff outside the unit, should not anticipate sudden improvements in morale and efficiency when he/she announces the implementation of a liberal new practice with respect to permissible channels of communication. Many of the staff will be bewildered by the change and others will be unable to follow successfully the new instructions. Few individuals can be instructed to be innovative and to work independently and then comply with those instructions. Planned changes of this sort should be made gradually. Some workers may be unable to accept a less closely monitored work environment and may wish to transfer to more highly structured jobs.

When a serials manager has been able to decentralize communication channels, he/she is then free to develop critically important leadership skills. While the serials staff may communicate freely, the unit manager is not then relieved of responsibility for informing the staff of new developments or policies and practices. In a study of communication and satisfaction in organizations, Marrett and others suggested that negative views of work associates are likely to result if the direction of informal communication is upward, that is, from subordinates to superiors. If informal communication is downward, from superiors to subordinates, workers are more likely to have positive views of work associates. Most importantly, the researchers found that when there is intensive and well scheduled communication activity, workers are likely to have positive views of their work.[2]

Contrary to popular belief, therefore, regularly scheduled meetings do appear to serve a useful purpose. This study suggests that the serials manager should not only make consistent efforts to communicate information to the serials staff informally but should also plan scheduled meetings to share information and to discuss common concerns.

The serials manager has, in addition, a further responsibility for firm and decisive leadership. In a study of leadership styles in research and development or high technology organizations, Phillip Sadler identified four leadership styles:

1. The "tells" style in which the manager makes all decisions independently and expects his staff to accept them without question.
2. The "sells" style in which the manager makes all decisions independently but tries to persuade his staff to accept them.
3. The "consults" style in which the manager makes decisions based upon advice and suggestions from the staff.
4. The "joins" style in which the manager delegates decision-making to the staff.

Some managers in Sadler's study exhibited a fifth style best described as lacking any identifiable characteristics at all.

Sadler's results reaffirmed earlier research which had demonstrated a preference by the majority of workers for the consultative style of leadership. Workers has more confidence in managers who employed leadership techniques characteristic of this particular style than in managers whom workers perceived as utilizing techniques associated with any of the other styles. Workers also rated consultative managers highest in efficiency.

One unexpected result was the discovery that "leaders who are seen as having distinct and identifiable styles of leadership are more effective in promoting confidence and satisfaction, whatever style they adopt, than those who do not have a distinctive style." Sadler suggests that consistent behavior on the part of a manager allows his staff to know where it stands with him and to predict his actions and reactions. Managers whose management style cannot be identified by their subordinates are viewed as weak, indecisive, inconsistent, and incompetent.[3]

These findings suggest that serials managers, who also supervise skilled and generally well-educated, or educationally motivated people, similar to those in Sadler's study, should strive to develop a consultative style of management. There is, however, good news for those serials managers who may have difficulty in adopting this style. If they haven't been successful in developing or maintaining a consultative style of management, they should strive for consistency in adopting one of the other styles and in making that style as distinctive as possible.

Clerks, Paraprofessionals and Professionals

A sensitive serials manager will recognize that not all non-MLS holders in a serials unit are equivalent in training, experience and responsibility. Some beginning serials clerks will be assigned routine tasks, involving dull, repetitive work without much opportunity to exercise individual creativity and imagination. On the other hand, highly skilled paraprofessionals with many years of experience in library processing or public service will be involved in work which would challenge the talent and intellect of the most highly educated professional librarian.

Clerical workers assigned routine tasks will require different supervisory techniques to encourage them to remain in the serials unit than will paraprofessionals who have jobs that they consider intrinsically interesting. Some of these techniques are outlined later in this essay. In addition, in the best of all possible worlds, clerks in entry-level jobs would recognize that it would be possible for them to advance within the serials unit and become paraprofessionals.

To support this perception on the part of clerical workers, the special skills and experience of paraprofessionals should be explicitly recognized by serials managers. Paraprofessionals should be consulted in planning for changes or innovations in the serials unit and should be fully informed of any administrative plans.

Each serials manager knows at least one individual who has worked in serials processing or public service units for many years, who has a wide acquaintance with serial publications, local processing practices and user needs but who has never earned an M.L.S. Such individuals have, however, earned the respect of their colleagues and the right to special recognition by their unit managers.

Logically, the next concern must center around the necessity for a serials manager to possess the M.L.S. degree. If an M.L.S. is not a basic prerequisite for successful supervision in a serials unit, why should this specific professional master's degree be essential for serials management? Why not a degree in art, management or nutrition? What basic skills should a serials manager have and how does graduate study in librarianship aid in the acquisition of these skills?

Each serials manager should strive to understand not only his or her own library's processing network but should be familiar with others, similar or disparate, so that the home situation can be understood better. A manager should be able to view serials operations objectively and realize that there are many different ways of accomplishing the same tasks. Management of the serials unit should be placed in the context of the library's mission, of the community of which it is a part and of the nationwide library community. Serials managers should be familiar with the serials collections in their own libraries and recognize their value to the user community. Serials managers must be able to administer their units, to read widely in the literature of the serials management field, to develop and maintain professional relationships, and to maintain an awareness of the universe of serial publications.

All of these responsibilities can be accomplished by serials managers without the M.L.S. but the specific training provided by graduate study in librarianship enables serials managers to perform this juggling act most effectively. M.L.S. holders will have had concentrated academic training in bringing together practical knowledge and research in a number of fields: management, librarianship, serials management, and specific academic subjects.

How many professional librarians are needed in a serials unit beyond the unit's manager? The answer to this question will depend upon the size of the unit. The organization charts of some of the smallest units with but a single librarian might topple over with the addition of one other librarian. In larger units, a serials manager may not be able to monitor effectively the unit's activities alone and another librarian may be essential.

Some serials units will have librarian specialists, depending upon the processing or public service activities for which a unit is responsible. For example, a serials unit may include catalogers, an exchanges librarian, public service desk supervisors, data conversion supervisors, selectors or acquisitions supervisors. Any of these jobs may also be held by serials unit workers without an M.L.S. The variety is endless and each serials manager will favor the arrangement in his/her unit as the best one. It is extraordinarily difficult to review the organization of many different serials processing and public service units and extrapolate a general theory about the most effective paraprofessional/librarian ratio in any such unit.

Almost any single serials task will be performed by non-M.L.S. holders in one library or another across the United States. It would appear, therefore, that except for general management of a serials unit and for assignment of those highly specialized tasks which a library administration thinks are best handled by professional librarians, most serials unit tasks and responsibilities can be turned over to non-M.L.S. holders. Library technicians can handle the most complex of tasks and problems solving, training, supervision and workflow monitoring. In the absence of any research on this subject, it may be suggested that professional librarians should be appointed only to those positions which involve over-all management along with the most highly specialized responsibilities.

Scattering professional librarians as sparsely as possible in a serials unit has an additional benefit. When budget cutters are looking for ways to economize and for departments to eliminate, the obvious places to begin are in those units with many highly paid, under-utilized librarians. Those units that are operating efficiently with many paraprofessionals and few librarians are more likely to be spared the heavy blows of the budgetary axe.

Staff Retention and Attrition

An area of concern which is related to both the economic and technological changes facing all of us is that of staff retention and attrition. Much attention has been given in the management literature to staff development in recent years but little or none has been given to the specific techniques which might be effective in serials departments in retaining staff and reducing the effects of natural attrition.

If one were to ask a library administrator, or even some serials managers, to identify the most expensive resource in a serials unit, the respondent might well identify computer hardware, manual or machine-readable files or computer-assisted processing systems.

The most expensive resource in a serials unit is, most clearly, its staff, with its cumulated years of training and experience. If a serials worker, with ten years of experience, resigns from the staff, the library loses an asset in which it has invested ten years of his salary payments, the salaries paid to his trainers or supervisors, the fees spent on in-service training courses or academic courses, as well as funds spent on other employee benefits and perquisites.

A serials unit worker assigned the most basic of clerical tasks may require a training period of three to six months before a minimal level of competency is achieved. Supervisors may require apprenticeships lasting a year or more. The vast knowledge of serials publishing, publication patterns, subscription agents and business practices which an experienced serials worker possesses is acquired over a period of years. For a single mid-level worker, without much supervisory responsibility, a library's investment over a five to seven year period could easily exceed $100,000.00. The entire costly training process must be repeated when a worker resigns and a replacement is hired.

Serials units are notorious for high employee turnover and for a high percentage of personnel problems.[4] How can a serials manager mitigate this tendency? Employee attrition can't be eliminated since people will inevitably decide to change careers, to move to Florida or to travel abroad. These decisions are beyond the power of any serials manager to prevent or curtail. They are a part of the modern American lifestyle.

A realistic serials manager can, however, plan for them. In recruiting for entry-level positions, primarily clerical in nature, serials managers ought to identify and hire candidates who will not be content to remain in those positions but who will soon demand more responsibility. A serials manager who follows this practice may find that even though the unit's entry-level positions turn over more often than they might if candidates with more limited aspirations were hired, the efficiency in the department doesn't suffer as a consequence. As senior staff members leave to conquer new worlds, junior staff members, familiar with the library's collections, its users and staff, and with departmental procedures are prepared to take their places.

Cross-training, that is, training a staff member assigned to one subunit to do a job in another subunit, can also be a helpful strategy in alleviating the problems resulting from high attrition. Cross-training enables staff to qualify for other jobs in the serials unit as these jobs are vacated. Individuals who do not presently have a primary assignment in a given subunit may also develop an interest in a particular job through cross-training opportunities.

When a department is fully staffed, cross-training provides variety in jobs that may have become routine or dull. In addition, it also gives workers a clearer understanding of the ways in which each job relates to the entire serials processing network in a library. For example, public services staff assigned to work in technical services jobs will develop a new and better understanding of the difficulty in persuading a publisher to send two copies of a journal for one year rather than one copy for two years. They'll also understand how renewal notices can bury themselves and remain undetected for months. On the other hand, technical services staff, directly confronted with readers' demands for service and materials immediately, and not later, will understand better the pressure facing public service staff every day.

When vacancies or illnesses occur, staff trained to work in other areas of a serials unit may be called on to assist temporarily in the subunits affected. Admittedly, some tasks may be left undone. In an imperfect organization, the serials manager must decide which tasks are most important and which can be left undone, or partially done, for an interim period. While cross-training cannot be considered an adequate substitute for a sufficiently large staff to accomplish all of the work to be done, it will enable a serials manager to shift a unit's staff to functions or tasks which are the most essential ones.

Finally, a cross-training can provide an interim solution to a sudden reduction in staff assigned to a serial unit. If individuals have been trained to work in more than one subunit or at tasks other than their primary assignments, they may be quickly reassigned to areas of greatest need. Everyone, staff, serials manager and library administrators, should understand that some tasks must be left undone until staffing is brought up to previous levels or until permanent decisions are made concerning tasks or services which will be eliminated or reduced in scope.

In addition to cross-training, an active staff development program can be utilized as a technique for encouraging staff to remain in a serials unit. It will also serve to reduce the impact on the unit when the inevitable resignations occur.

The best serials workers have good analytical minds, well-developed oral and written skills and a keen interest in solving complex problems. Workers of this caliber generally want to continue their occupational or professional development and may have outside academic interests that they also wish to pursue. In developing plans to retain such valuable workers, a serials manager ought to be concerned with assisting them to fulfill as many of their educational goals as is practical.

To many managers, staff development implies a formal program initiated by a personnel officer which will take workers away from their desks for long periods of time. Other managers may view staff development as training given a worker so that individual can successfully complete assigned tasks. For instance, training to search a bibliographic data base in order to do bibliographic checking might be regarded as staff development.

To the contrary, a manager who sets aside worktime for workers to learn skills which must be acquired to complete assigned tasks is not conducting a staff development program. Staff development ought, rather, to imply an ongoing program of practical training or education to acquire skills or knowledge which is not essential to the successful performance of a worker's basic assignment. Some aspects of a program may involve formal instruction and some time away from assigned work but may also involve informal learning opportunities within a serials unit. Cross-training is one example of such an opportunity. Tours or lectures conducted by an expert in one subspecialty for those who work in another, is another example.

Formal instruction conducted away from the serials work area may improve a worker's performance upon her return. Classes in personnel policies and procedures and in good supervisory methods are obvious examples of such worthwhile classes. Other possible staff development activities are classes in data processing or in computer programming in order to understand better how an automated serials system works; classes in a particular subject field in order to understand better the needs of the library's clientele working in a particular field; or classes in graphics in order to design better manuals, instruction sheets, pamphlets or signs.

Library time spent by a serials worker in acquiring new skills or knowledge benefits the worker but also benefits the library. It gains a well-trained, competent, enthusiastic staff member who is less likely to look for job satisfaction outside the serials unit. Library administrators would be horrified if expensive equipment were not well maintained and if obsolete equipment were not replaced. A library's financial investment in its staff far exceeds that in its equipment and is far more difficult to replace or renovate, once workers have resigned or have allowed their skills to become obsolescent. A library's workers should be considered its most valuable assets. Their skills should be continually improved, their knowledge of technological advancements maintained, and their academic interests developed.

Economic Gloom Ahead

What's a serials manager to do when positions are frozen, staff is assigned to other departments or units and subscription lists are trimmed? The time to begin anticipating these crises is about two years before they occur. The same strategies will be useful after crises occur but will be much more difficult to implement. All of the strategies used for staff retention and for effective communication and leadership can be utilized effectively to minimize the impact of budget cuts.

An enthusiastic and innovative staff may frequently suggest redundant or superfluous tasks that might be eliminated. The key to receiving such suggestions is to have employed staff workers who are imaginative and independent and who might well qualify for jobs elsewhere in the library world or in the public or private sectors yet who prefer to work in a serials unit. These preferences may arise from the joy of working with serial publications but most often arise from more selfish and, some would say, more trustworthy motivations. The freedom to work independently; to develop new processing routines; to work with serials vendors; to gain expertise in a particular aspect of library processing; to have a flexible work schedule to pursue academic studies or alternate career interests; or to combine child rearing with paid employment: these are but a few of the reasons workers may choose to remain in a serials unit.

Few of these busy individuals will choose to spend their entire careers in serials work or even in libraries. They do, however, bring to critical situations novel viewpoints, as well as intelligence, dedication to problem resolution and a willingness to try a different approach and to take risks. They are also less fearful of change and less attached to the *status quo*. In a climate of radical change, these staff members will be able to cope with great transformations and devise new techniques for overcoming any adverse consequences associated with modifications in library policies, practices and approaches.

In response to budgetary restrictions, there has been a highly visible trend in libraries in recent years to rearrange organizational patterns according to the functions performed rather than according to the formats of the materials processed, housed or circulated. The contest rages on with valid arguments presented for both points of view. This discussion, limited to staffing of serials units, will stress those arguments which favor maintaining some kind of serials unit intact.

If subscription lists are reduced, library administrators may feel justified in reducing the size of the staff devoted to serials processing or public service. In the past decade, when subscriptions lists have dropped below 10,000 titles, serials departments have vanished in some libraries. The serials staff has been absorbed by acquisitions, cataloging and public service units. Some librarians, primarily non-serials managers, have been satisfied with the results and pleased with the added flexibility offered. Serials managers, to the contrary, have not been uniformly pleased and have suggested that the serials collections and services will deteriorate as staff specifically trained to handle serials processing and services leave the library staff. One might argue that, if reductions to current subscription lists are proportionally greater than the reductions in clientele served, the use of the remaining titles will increase and closer attention to maintenance of the serials collection would be mandatory. While a smaller staff would be required to manage a collection of 10,000 titles than a collection of 20,000 or 25,000, a serials unit ought, nevertheless to continue to exist in order to maintain the collection. This unit may be a department or a subunit within a department. The critical factor is the provision of specialized training and the utilization of the experience and interests of the staff maintaining the serials collection in both processing and public service areas. The serials collection in academic and research libraries and in some large public libraries is the *heart* of the library collection. Special, or rare, collections may endow a library with prestige but are not the bread and butter materials on which good public service is based. The public service staff must rely on an enthusiastic, concerned and dedicated processing staff to maintain a library's serials collection. If the processing staff is indifferent or uninformed, public service must inevitably suffer.

Automation as Remedy

In many libraries, emphasis given to computer-assisted materials processing and public service responsibilities looms hugely and expensively. Some library administrators look at the apparently magical properties of automation and decide that this balm, once applied, will solve all of a library's existing problems.

Automation is not a cure-all, however. A library with serious morale, competency, organizational or other kinds of grave and global problems in its serials processing and public service units, must resolve these problems before embarking on a major data conversion or processing conversion project. Attempts to automate around a set of problems will serve only to superimpose an additional layer of automation-related problems on unresolved organizational and staff problems. Radical changes of any sort put great stress on an organization and exacerbate pre-existing problems. Existing staff distress or unhappiness is likely to prevent successful implementation of a computer-assisted processing or public access system.

A poorly organized staff, with an inefficient workflow, poor rapport with a library's clientele and badly structured jobs will not be miraculously transformed by the mystique of automation into an efficiently-organized, well-run unit. A library plagued by any or all of these conditions should resolve them before embarking on the treacherous path to automation. The journey will be difficult enough without the addition of serious handicaps. A poorly trained, badly motivated and unhappy staff can effectively sabotage the implementation of a new computer-assisted system.

Even the best-motivated and most enthusiastic of serials unit staffs will be concerned about the uncertainties of an automated future. Serials unit staff members who are distrustful of management's motives prior to automation will not be won over by the dramatic improvements in information retrieval which will result from automation of various manual processes.

A certain unevenness in the operation of a new system is to be expected: records are omitted from the conversion process or are badly bungled; essential items of information are omitted; and essential processing tasks are forgotten in the design of the new computer-assisted system. There may be program bugs, difficulties with hardware, or problems with delivery of equipment or supplies. All of these difficulties may be overcome successfully if the staff is willing to be flexible, innovative and patient and to explain to library users the temporary nature of the difficulties with access to records. Few of these minor problems will be overcome if the staff is despondent, unenthusiastic, bitter and anxious.

Analysis of the Manual System

Having completed a critical examination of staff morale and enthusiasm, library managers and administrators who are satisfied that their staff is productive and well-motivated must then face the daunting task of reorganizing processing and, perhaps, public service units to accommodate computer-assisted processing and public service activities.

Analysis of the existing organizational structure is an important prerequisite to restructuring a serials unit to accommodate automation. Before a computer-assisted processing system can be effectively utilized, serials managers must know what operations or procedures will be altered and what effects on processing or public services may be anticipated. In describing the existing manual system, the process of making change acceptable to the staff begins. If the serials unit staff is fully involved, each staff member will be permitted to arrive at his/her own realization that some operations will be obsolete, that many procedures or files are inconsistent, and that certain tasks are left undone while other, less essential, jobs are done twice over.

In some libraries, there has been a tendency to think that the manual system should be automated with every minute procedure left intact. The staff may insist that all of the little wrinkles and idiosyncrasies of the manual system must be faithfully replicated in the computer-assisted system. Examination of the manual system's staffing pattern and operations, with the serials staff conducting the review, will be useful in determining which aspects of the manual system should be replicated and which portions may be eliminated or modified.

Many serials units are organized around major files. For example, the mail receipt and claiming subunit will have major responsibility for the receiving files and will be the major users of those files. Bindery preparation subunits will have major responsibility for the maintenance of the bindery files and will be the primary users of those files. In developing a computer-assisted system, the serials units manager may discover that the information which filled a multitude of manual files will be compressed into a single centralized automated file. Gone will be the redundancy that necessitated library staff to accept discrepancies in the information found in various files. Differences in choice and form of main entries, in the beginning date of a library's file of a particular serials title, or in records of missing volumes or issues will no longer bewilder serials workers and library users. The need for repetition of information among a number of files will vanish. It will no longer be necessary for typist after typist to repeat the same items of information for a single serial title in file after file.

When multiple files disappear, then some of the traditional divisions among various aspects of serials work may also vanish. Identification of volumes ready for binding may take place at the point of receipt rather than at the final shelving location. A virtually complete record for a title that has been ordered may be keyed into the machine-readable file by acquisitions staff. When service begins, cataloging staff will add only classification, subject headings and make other minor adjustments to the record. Staff who were formerly experts in one aspect of serials processing or public service may become experts in different aspects or in many more aspects.

As file redundancy vanishes, many procedures and tasks may become obsolete or redundant as well. If no one on the serials staff can recall why a certain operation or procedure is part of the workflow, it becomes an obvious candidate for elimination. It is vital, however, for the serials staff to be involved in work-flow alterations, in developing a new organizational structure and in modifying individual job descriptions. Even the most analytically gifted members of a serials unit's staff will tend to cling to tasks which they have accepted as the only right and proper ways to accomplish certain processing or public service objectives.

Yet if these staff members are involved in determining which changes will be made and in implementing those changes, they are much more likely to accept them and to make them work effectively.

In addition, serials staff may also be able to present cogent arguments concerning the importance of retaining a certain type of record or item of information in the computer-assisted serials system.

External Vs. Internal Change Agents

An important component of the development of any computer-assisted system will be provision for training in new procedures and techniques and for preparation of written manuals. Many serials units are minimally staffed so that supervisors are generally required to handle a full workload in addition to training, supervising, monitoring workflow and preparing manuals. In planning for automation, efforts should be made by serials managers to transfer a large portion of supervisors' routine work assignments to others so that they will have time for training, writing manuals and similar activities. There is no simple formula for reorganization so that these functions may be highlighted and given the importance required in an age of rapid technological change. While adding staff to the serials unit may be a theoretical alternative, it is rarely a practical option in any library. A partial solution may be found in delegating more work to junior staff members or in suspending some routine tasks assigned to supervisors.

Another, less desirable alternative is to appoint outside consultants to train staff and write procedures. These individuals may come from personnel offices, computer centers, or consulting firms, or they may be senior library staff without primary assignments.

In response to this solution, one author has noted that those organizational development projects which failed have certain characteristics in common. Among them is the use of change agents who were not part of the organization being studied. Those projects which were successful selected internal change agents; that is, individuals who were already working in the organization and so were responsible for engineering change with greater care than did the unsuccessful projects. Change agents in successful projects had well-developed problem identification and problem resolution skills. In addition, these internal change agents were given primary responsibility for managing change, while in unsuccessful projects, external agents were assigned that responsibility.[5] This analysis suggests that library administrators would be well-advised to delegate responsibility for development and implementation of a computer-assisted processing and public access system to carefully selected members of the serials unit's staff.

There is additional reason, in most libraries, for utilizing internal change agents. Most libraries have organization charts and procedures manuals but most of these are sadly outdated and inaccurate. In many libraries, it would be a mistake to rely on these out-of-date-information sources to examine the current organization and to plan for modifications. Those who are best able to describe an organization are those who work within it. Serials managers will find that interviews conducted by themselves or by other senior staff will be an effective method of determining the actual organizational structure and relationships in a unit. It may require some practice for each individual to describe accurately his own job and the ways in which he interacts with other individuals. Patience and persistence will be required on the part of the interviewer. An outside consultant or interviewer anxious to complete an organizational study may miss vital tasks. An interviewer from within an organizational unit will know when all tasks, functions and responsibilities have been described and will know when a search must be made for a missing element.

A Computer-Assisted Oligarchy

In developing a new organizational structure in response to implementation of a computer-assisted processing and information system, library administrators often insist on assigning primary responsibility to a small corps of individuals who will be able to maintain the system without assistance from the remainder of the staff. These individuals are assigned to develop the system, to write manuals and to train others in all aspects of the system.

With a new toy in the library, administrators may allow a few favored individuals to play with it, denying this pleasure to other, less favored, staff members. Reasons behind this approach have a certain surface validity. The system is often perceived as difficult to operate and maintain and only the most capable of staff members will be able to use it and understand it. Library administration and management will not want to perpetuate the problems of the old manual system in the age of automation. The computer-assisted system may be in a developmental phase at present and training all staff to use it is seen as inefficient use of the valuable time of system developers. There's so much developmental work still to be done, argue these administrators, and there is so little time to train the staff. These are all easily defended reasons for confining development and implementation of the computer-assisted system to a few individuals and for delaying the training of the majority of the staff until the new system is stable.

What are some of the consequences of this policy decision? Formerly competent staff members who are not part of the elite group become demoralized. They are no longer masters of their craft but have been demoted to a status below that of an apprentice. They remain in the serials unit, struggling to maintain processing or public service standards, without a clear understanding of the effects of the new computer-assisted system. The future efficiency of the serials unit in which manual and automated systems must operate in tandem for the indefinite future is jeopardized since that portion of the serials staff trained only to operate the manual system is ignorant of the computer-assisted system. It will be difficult for the outgroup workers to train incoming staff in the use and maintenance of both the existing manual and new computer-assisted processing systems.

System planners or developers lose the benefits of the collective wisdom and experience of serials workers who are not part of the select group. In some large and complex libraries, there is a strong likelihood of failing to take into account certain vital aspects of any serials processing and information system in designing and developing a computer-assisted system. For instance, system designers, unfamiliar with serials acquisitions practices, may fail to include the name and address of a periodical publisher on a purchase order if the order is being placed with a subscription agent. They may not realize that billing and shipping address for serials subscriptions may differ or that it is important to record information about the receipt of duplicate issues.

Effective implementation and utilization of the computer-assisted system may be seriously impaired since the serials staff will not have been encouraged to consider the computer-assisted system one of its own working tools. The new system, expensive and technologically advanced as library administrators and managers may consider it, is still merely a tool to assist the serials unit staff and others to put issues into the hands of library users.

Another counter productive option that some library administrators may consider is to move the existing staff into non-essential positions, to encourage early retirement or to urge them to seek jobs in libraries that have not automated. Some staff may be terminated because their skills are considered obsolete. They ignore the fact that new staff brought in to operate the computer-assisted system will not have had the training, skills, experience, detailed knowledge of serial publications, or of a library's particular needs and constraints that the former, pre-automation staff possessed.

Today's computer technology is developing rapidly and becoming easier to use by the month so that any reasonably intelligent serials worker should be able to master the operation of a computer-assisted processing system with ease. In some instances, serials unit supervisors may discover that it is far easier to train new workers to interpret machine-generated records than to decipher hand-written records on smudged 3 x 5 or 4 x 7 cards.

Conclusion

Many serials managers are optimists and believe that perfection lies just around the corner or that the ultimate solution to staffing problems or inadequacies will be discovered in the near future. Realistic serials management in the eighties must, however, include the certain knowledge that effective management will consist largely of adaptation to changing circumstances and that perfection will elude us all.

Use of special techniques to recruit and retain productive staff, to create efficient and cooperative serials processing or public services groups, or to minimize the negative aspects and increase the positive benefits of automation emerge from a management approach which stresses flexibility and awareness of rapid economic and technological changes.

The optimism of each serials manager should lie in the belief that a solution to each staffing crisis or problem can be found if sufficient ingenuity is focused on the situation. No solution can be considered permanent, but if sufficient foresight has been exercised, earlier solutions may aid in the resolution of future problems.

NOTES

1. Joseph H. Reitz. *Behavior in Organizations* (Homewood, IL: Irwin, 1977), p. 351–353.

2. Cora B. Marrett, Jerald Hage and Michael Aiken. "Communication and Satisfaction in Organizations," *Human Relations*, 28:7 (1975), p. 619, 622.

3. Philip J. Sadler. "Leadership Style, Confidence in Management, and Job Satisfaction," *Journal of Applied Behavioral Science*, 6:1 (1970), p. 3–19.

4. David Taylor. "Gremlin Theory of Serial Title Changes," *Title Varies*, 4:4–6 (1977), p. 38.

5. Jerome L. Franklin. "Characteristics of Successful and Unsuccessful Organization Development," *Journal of Applied Behavioral Science*, 12:4 (1976), p. 483, 487.

AACR2 AND SERIAL RECORDS

Wilma Reid Cipolla

The impact of the code will be especially disruptive to serials. Just at the time when the CONSER data base has been developed and serials union list activity is expanding, AACR2 will cause major problems.[1]

To librarians engaged in the management of serials, the above statement may be an understatement. Significant alterations to cataloging principles, while difficult to implement for monographic publications, have serious consequences when applied to continuing titles. In contrast to monographs, serials are intended to be published indefinitely, in the course of which they may change title, issuing body, publisher, numbering scheme, and/or merge with, be absorbed by, or split into other serials. Each change in bibliographic data in turn produces modifications to a large array of related serial files, the nature and extent of which vary from institution to institution.

Change being nothing new to serials librarians, why should the adoption of the second edition of the *Anglo-American Cataloguing Rules*[2] be such an important issue? The reasons are numerous and interrelated. One can cite the "document explosion" and the dramatic impact it has had on serial publications. Reliance on nationwide data bases, both as sources for catalog copy and as cooperative finding tools, compels catalogers more than ever before to implement rules in a similar, if not identical, manner. Since AACR1 was applied to serials "with a wide degree of intentional variation,"[3] incompatibility between existing records is a common condition, making resolution of conflicts caused by the new code particularly difficult. In addition, the general adoption of AACR2 according to a common timetable, in contrast to the piecemeal application of AACR1, is forcing libraries into the decision-making mode immediately, with little option for exercising the "wait and see," or experience, method. The issue is further complicated, at least initially, by the availability of new filing rules,[4] obligating the library world to consider, if not deal with, two changes at once.

But what is it about the code that will be so disruptive? The answer lies, in part, in how serials librarians handle what Osborn calls "the principle of complementary records."[5] Unlike a monograph, for which there is only one bibliographic record (albeit with multiple access points), a serial which is received on a subscription basis, renewed annually, and bound regularly, requires a number of files, usually of the single-entry type, to achieve adequate management of each process. The method of bibliographic control is centered therefore not on the library catalog, but on a variety of complementary records which may be characterized as semibibliographic in nature. These supporting records are often not controlled by the cataloger, but by a mixture of professional and clerical staff with little or no knowledge of cataloging rules and sometimes limited expertise with serials themselves. Unfortunately, the energy devoted by the profession to standardization of cataloging rules has had no similar counterpart, at least until recently, in efforts toward uniformity in the construction and format of order, receipt, payment, claim, binding, and union list records.[6] Osborn's landmark work notwithstanding, current practice in serials management can be said to have developed largely through local tradition and personal experience.[7]

Types of Records

At the risk of restating the obvious, it might be useful to review the broad spectrum of record-keeping functions embraced by the rubric "serial records." In some institutions the serial record is limited to the check-in function and may be restricted to periodicals. In other libraries the term, sometimes expressed as the Central Serial Record, may encompass not only receipt and payment records, but also acquisitions, catalog, union list, and/or binding files. Differing policies regarding classification of serials affect both the number and types of bibliographic records controlling continuing titles. There is considerable variation in the extent of centralization and duplication of serial records, especially in larger institutions, as well as in their availability for public use. For the purposes of this discussion "serial records" will be defined as any record which maintains control over a technical processing operation, and will be confined to traditional manual records. Experience with on-line serials systems is still so meagre that the ramifications of AACR2 cannot be adequately addressed in this essay.[8]

Receipt records normally handle check-in and claiming, but often include the closely-related order and payment functions. These records may be maintained in a single file for all categories of serials (including newspapers, looseleaf services, monographic series, etc.), or

divided into several files, perhaps in different departments. Classified materials may be segregated from unclassified. There may be separate files for microforms, documents, gift and exchange titles, memberships, blanket orders, non-retained and vertical file serials, and cross-references. Acquisitions may be administered through the receiving process, or controlled through individual files for new orders, new order claims, received orders, and cancelled orders. Check-in records which handle subscription and standing order claims, plus invoicing, have related claim, address, and correspondence files, along with financial records. In some libraries the Kardex is the locus of binding activity, and in turn may constitute the holdings record for bound periodicals. If the official accession file is not available to public service staff, or branches maintain their own records, there may be visible files in the reference area or reading room. Shelving devices are also necessary to look after current journals.

Full cataloging, with production of complete card sets and holdings records, is sometimes given only to those titles which are classified. Other categories of serials may not have any catalog cards at all, or they may be represented by brief bibliographic records, from which class numbers, added entries, and/or subject headings are omitted. Serial cards can be interfiled with the main public or union catalog, or else kept together in a separate serials catalog for public and technical services use. A "union" or serials list might be the only means of public access to continuing titles. Such listings vary as to the extent of coverage, often including only one class of publications, such as periodicals, and are frequently limited to currently received titles. Union lists can be in typed, printed, computer printout, or COM format, and could emanate from a cooperative agency or be solely an in-house tool.

Frequency of production is highly variable, ranging from the immediacy of the on-line lists which are currently being developed, to regular updates or infrequent revisions. Recording and maintenance of serial holdings data could take place in any number of catalogs or shelf lists, as well as in the Kardex, union list, or binding file.

Catalog Options

Before launching into a discussion of the impact of the new rules on this diverse body of records, it would be well to highlight the basic changes affecting serials. First, there is no longer a "special rule on main entry for serials;" and second, the concept of corporate authorship has been superseded by "a rigorous operational definition of corporate responsibility,"[9] or in the language of the code, corporate "emanation" (Rule 21.1B2). Use of corporate names as access points is now restricted to five specific categories, resulting in more title main entries and in changes from corporate body entry to title entry. The rules for form of entry prescribe use of the name by which the body is predominantly known (Rule 24.1), producing altered forms of corporate entry, particularly in those institutions which followed LC's practice of superimposition in applying AACR-1. Chapter 25 deals with uniform titles, a concept which is being expanded by LC to include serials, as a means of distinguishing between titles that are the same.[10] Formulation of geographic qualifiers (Rule 23.1) may change the form of name, both corporate and uniform title. The rules for description, which employ the ISBD(S) framework,[11] for choice of elements, order, and punctuation, can also affect local convention for format and construction of serial records other than catalog cards. Depending on library policies regarding successive vs. latest-entry cataloging, the guidelines given in Rules 21.2 and 21.3 for changes in titles proper and corporate bodies may impact on numerous linking records.

Implementation of AACR2 presents little or no problem for new titles with no previous publication history or association with titles already in the collection. The difficulties arise when cataloging or recataloging titles associated with serials already represented in the catalog under earlier rules. They could be works related bibliographically through title changes, or publications related by common issuing body or series tracing. Assuming a library makes the decision to apply the new rules, what are the possibilities for accommodating these changes to serials in the card catalog?

The five options described by Jean Decker in 1979[12] had resolved themselves by January 1981 basically into two alternatives: keep the catalog open and maintain one file consisting of both AACR2 and pre-AACR2 records; or close the old catalog and start a new, all-AACR2 catalog.[13] Both options have several possible solutions for implementation, with the prime difference being the extent of correction employed to resolve conflicts between new and existing records and materials. Correction in this context is defined as reformatting, recataloging, refiling, rebinding, remarking, and/or reshelving. Other means of accommodation might include shifting of files or providing of cross-references without revision. Corrective action can be applied to one or a combination of the three major aspects of change — choice of entry, form of entry, and description[14] — and can be limited to files under a certain size.

Specific solutions can range all the way from correcting all serials to conform to AACR2, through converting only those records in conflict with AACR2, down to cataloging new serials (including those resulting from some bibliographic change) as AACR2 while retaining pre-AACR2 records for all or a portion of any titles linked to the new title. The solutions employing maximum correction will produce the most unified files; those with less must accept the existence of split files for serial holdings.[15]

Management Problems

Selection of an option for the catalog represents only one stage of the decision-making process for the serials librarian. Aside from such general considerations as collection size, quality of service, cost, and resources, the variables unique to serial records and serials processing make the choice particularly complex. The issue of conflict between records is of acute importance when any one of the following conditions exists:
1. numerous files, either unique or duplicate, controlling serials;
2. inconsistent treatment of titles, depending on category of publication, as in collections where annuals are classified but periodicals are not;
3. decentralized responsibility for bibliographic control combined with centralized public access to serial holdings, as in large systems with several autonomous cataloging and processing units.

Think, for a moment, of the difficulties faced with multiple publications of a given association or body (such as the Association for Computing Machinery, or Standard & Poor's) for which titles cataloged prior to January 1981 were entered and bound under corporate body, but for which new publications or title changes will very likely be entered under title according to AACR2. In a collection of any size, the amount of correction necessary to provide a unified file would be formidable. But how would orders, check-in, union list, and binding be coordinated with split files?

Should orders for new publications be placed under title, but under corporate body when ordering added subscriptions, replacements, or back volumes for titles cataloged under earlier rules? Should there be see-references in the check-in file for those publications entered under title, or should all titles be filed together regardless of catalog entry? Should there be see-also references in the union list to insure that users find all publications issued by a given association? Should "dummies" or "shelved-in" notes be employed to direct the browser to titles now shelved in different places?

Consider further the problem presented if periodicals in microform are classified and represented in the union catalog, but the same title in hard copy is not. What if a microform received and cataloged after January 1981 is for an earlier manifestation of the title currently being received in hard copy? Should the entry for the microform be established according to AACR1 to be consistent with other

57

catalog records, or should it be cataloged according to AACR2 and all later titles recataloged, rebound or remarked, and reshelved?[16] Ponder yet another situation where one unit in a system cataloged a given title before 1981 and another unit adds the title to its collection after January 1981. If both are represented in the union list, should the first unit recatalog to be consistent with the second, or should the title be entered twice?

Strategy for Planning

The problems are clearly complex; the approach to their solution is equally involved. Basic to any consideration of accommodating AACR2 are these questions:
1. the volume of changes;
2. the nature of the changes;
3. the rate at which we will have to process them.[17]

Unique to serials records are four additional questions, which will be dealt with in turn.

Should the option of "open" vs. "closed" catalog be applied to all serial records?

A decision to close old files and begin new all-AACR2 files seems to be a remote possibility for serial records other than the card or book catalog.[18] If the goal for the "open" file is to bring all serials into conformance with AACR2, the quantity of material to be corrected will represent an enormous project. Even redoing records for all currently published or received titles is a formidable task, not to mention including retrospective links. There would be no identifiable benefit to having two files if titles added to the collection are the only ones in the new file, since each search would require a two-step process.[19] Regardless of the decision for the card catalog, the choice for other serial records seems clear — maintain a single file of AACR2 and pre-AACR2 records.

Can the specific solutions chosen for classified materials be followed for unclassified serials as well?

Once the decision is made to maintain single, "open" files, at least for non-catalog records, the choice between maximum and minimum correction will be at least partially determined by library policies on the classification of serials. If a large proportion of the collection is unclassified and shelved by title, routine processing of title changes and the addition of new titles will place the publications cataloged under AACR2 "out-of-pocket," both in the visible files and on the shelves. A decision to correct related records will require rebinding or remarking of spines, plus shifting of volumes in the stacks. The difficulty of carrying out these steps is compounded in libraries with open-shelf access to materials; this has an attendant problem of locating and controlling the inventory while correction is in process. Further, if all materials are controlled through a central serial record or union list, correction cannot be confined to only the title in hand. It must be extended to records for the same title in multiple copies and other formats.

Alternately, if all serials are normally classified, conversion of catalog records will affect only the order, check-in, and union list functions. Modification of volumes already bound would probably not be necessary, since the method of retrieval is not changed. Similarly, reshelving may be avoided by retaining original cutter numbers. A change in policy toward classification has been suggested as a way of mitigating the impact of AACR2,[20] but the choice "between revision and division"[21] still remains.

To how many titles and at what point in the publishing history or processing operation will the rules be applied?

At this point, a statistical study of the serials collection may be useful to try to determine how many titles may be converted to AACR2. The range of choices described earlier will be limited to revising only serials on subscription or standing order or those still being published, whether currently received or not. Volume of work might be further narrowed to cataloging begun after a certain point in time. When recataloging due to change in title proper or corporate body, a decision can be made to redo the previous title, or leave the earlier cataloging intact, adding only the necessary note to relate the two records. One should also consider the advisability of converting linking titles, particularly in older libraries where serials are represented by records done under a variety of cataloging codes and policies on successive vs. latest-entry cataloging.

The crucial factor here is the number of titles bibliographically linked together. This apparently has not been addressed in any published reports, but samples included in two unpublished studies indicate that for periodicals alone the number of linking entries requiring correction may range from almost 20 percent[22] to approximately 40 percent,[23] depending on whether the link to only the previous title or to the entire chain of title changes has been considered. This factor may well determine how far back in the publishing history to go. Given a situation in which there are inadequate records and unclassified volumes with improper spine titles, this might be the golden opportunity to upgrade the entire collection. If, however, the official records were properly formulated by the cataloging rules in force at the time, it may be expedient to leave all earlier titles alone and apply AACR2 to only the most recent title change.

Selection of points in the processing operation which are appropriate for initiation of record correction is highly dependent on local practice and resources. It may be that revision can be done as a mass conversion project and all necessary records corrected at once. Many libraries, however, will have to take a gradual approach and must then decide on which nodes in the system will trigger review for possible conflicts. It could start with check-in, be part of the added-volume routine, or wait until preparation of volumes for binding. Review might occur during the acquisitions process when orders are placed for added subscriptions or for volumes to fill in gaps in periodical runs. But if "the serials catalogers . . . function as the bibliographic authority for the Serials Department,"[24] then records are more properly scrutinized as part of the cataloging operation.

Any one of the following actions might initiate conversion to AACR2: recataloging due to chang in corporate body or title proper, editing records due to cessation or transfer, processing second copies or added volumes in the same or different format. If the cataloging staff is responsible for preparing and correcting check-in or union list records, then cancellations and reinstatements will also prompt needed changes. Unclassified periodical titles which have never been bound may force either examination of present records or preparation of such where none exist. Serials catalogers responsible for monographic series and series authority work will themselves trigger numerous corrections in related serial files. It is essential, therefore, to make specific decisions on which categories will be corrected and which processing operations will initiate the correction. This is necessary if one is to control cataloging workflow and production and coordinate the total management of a serials collection.

Can or should all serial records be kept consistent with one another?

The practice of using catalog entry for the visible file is a long-standing one according to Osborn,[25] recommended by Smith,[26] and deemed "essential to effective serial treatment" at Berkeley.[27] Prior to the appearance of AACR2 though, other points of view surfaced, reflecting the debate over the problem of entry for serial publications. Gorman suggested that "it does not seem unreasonable . . . to prescribe one entry for integration in a general catalog and another for use as the basic entry in a serials list."[28] Chan, responding to Spalding's statement that check-in and storage of issues could be under title regardless of cataloging rules,[29] cautioned that "this would create a great discrepancy and inconsistency between serials records and cataloging entries . . . a situation which would no doubt cause other problems."[30] What are those other problems, and does the advent of new cataloging and filing rules solve them or make them worse?

First in order of consideration is the relationship between public access tools and technical services files. If all titles are controlled through a catalog with multiple access points and shelved by class numbers, consistency of entries between the catalog and check-in file may have little effect on use. Where access to holdings is maintained solely by means of a single-entry file, the presence of incompatibility will greatly trouble users following up on citations from the literature, inter-library loan staff armed with entries from the *National Union Catalog* or *New Serial Titles*, and patrons utilizing regional union lists.[31]

In libraries where all or part of the serial collection is shelved alphabetically and controlled through a combination of check-in, union list, and bindery files, then each must direct the user to the same title and one shelf location. Furthermore, the filing system in these various places should match that used for storage, especially in libraries with unrestricted access and/or limited reference service for serials. If the user is not being well-served now, AACR2 and the new filing rules may provide the impetus necessary to correct these inadequacies.

The second point — consistency among various technical services files — is more difficult to deal with, due to the lack of standardization in record format and arrangement. Keeping in mind Osborn's principle of complementary records, the problem can be approached by isolating two primary variables. First, the number of files which must be accessed by the staff in order to carry out their duties will determine how important it is to keep all related files consistent with regard to choice and form of entry. Consider, for instance, the invoice clerk who receives a bill citing order number only. How will the proper payment record be located? If the answer is the Received-Order-Record, then the entry in that file must match the one in the payment file.

In addition, filing rules which differ from one file to another can impair both efficiency and effectiveness of searching. A decision on the amount of correction to be undertaken should consider if consistency is crucial in carrying out such common activities as solving check-in problems by consulting the series authority file and public catalog, pre-order searching for second-copy or back-run requests in the union lists and check-in file, processing claims initiated by branch libraries, and answering reference inquiries channelled from the public catalog or union list.

Second, the amount of duplication necessary between records will be a factor in deciding on the need for consistency with regard to descriptive aspects of the code. Osborn feels that check-in and catalog records "should not be permitted to duplicate each other beyond a bare minimum,"[32] and that "the guiding principle [for union lists] should be to omit all nonessential data."[33] Although the question of duplication is certainly not unique with AACR2, the new code does force a reexamination of the primary purpose of each aspect of serials work. For check-in it is essential to match the piece in hand with its proper record; in this case, will inclusion of the publisher and place of publication as given in the first issue, even though it is no longer valid for current issues, be helpful or confusing?

Are such elements as parallel titles, other title information, and statement of responsibility necessary for identification of titles in the union list? Is ISBD punctuation appropriate for spine titles? Should uniform titles be used to distinguish between serials with the same title only in those files where there are conflicts? And if the cataloging staff is responsible for preparing other serial records, is it more efficient to duplicate the catalog records, or remember to eliminate certain elements for specific files?

The third problem may represent the most obvious impact of AACR2 on serial records. Lack of consistency within individual "open" files becomes painfully evident when rules are changed and can be highly confusing to public and library staff alike. Turner notes that "it will be difficult . . . for the proprietors of single-entry serials lists to explain to their users why some publications called simply *Journal* are entered under 'J' and others are entered under the name of the society or institution which is responsible for them."[34] The Michigan report pointed out that a central serial record with cross-references will make searching and recording more difficult and error-prone."[35] Filing problems will arise between old and new titles beginning with initialisms or acronyms. There will be discrepancies in both the Kardex and union list where series entries and uniform titles carry differing forms and types of qualifiers. Check-in clerks will be uncertain about retaining subtitles or non-ISBD punctuation when preparing replacement cards for pre-AACR2 records.

Summary

At this point it is in order to review the solutions advanced for the catalog and consider once again whether they are feasible for the rest of serial records. The decision between revision and division is critical, involving not only AACR2 but filing rules. Further, the question of an appropriate time frame for action is a serious one, affecting service and efficiency.

As I have noted earlier, planning to correct all serials or all curretly received or published titles will be a massive job. Even converting all titles in conflict with AACR2 will constitute a major operation. One might entertain the option of creating artificial successive entries, to avoid complete recataloging. If catalog corrections cannot be done, should the Kardex be refiled by title, and if so, what about the union list? Should documents be kept together under issuing body, regardless of catalog entry? Will cross-references be a better way of handling "out-of-pocket" titles or will staff be able to adapt to two-step searches? Can "tracings" be used in single-entry files? How will blind references be avoided? Should the union list be expanded to a multiple-access tool? How will AACR2-compatible records be tagged during a gradual conversion project?

The librarian who has progressed through this maze of decision making will surely agree that serials present formidable problems. This essay has attempted to identify specific areas where decisions are needed for the management of serial records under AACR2 and to suggest a strategy for planning. Clearly more questions have been raised than solutions proposed, but perhaps they may aid in preventing "loss of control . . . due to lack of good management."[36]

NOTES

1. Mary C. Hall, Response to solicitation of opinion on the costs and benefits of AACR2, *Alternative Catalog Newsletter* 21 (June 1980): 8.

2. *Anglo-American Cataloguing Rules*, 2d ed. (Chicago: American Library Association, 1978), hereafter referred to as AACR2 and cited by rule number as necessary.

3. John D. Byrum, Jr., and D. Whitney Coe, "*AACR* as Applied by Research Libraries for Serials Cataloging," *Library Resources and Technical Services* 23/2 (Spring 1979): 139.

4. *ALA Filing Rules*. (Chicago: American Library Association, 1980); and *Library of Congress Filing Rules*. (Washington, DC: Library of Congress, 1980).

5. Andrew D. Osborn. *Serial Publications*, 3d ed. (Chicago: American Library Association, 1980), p. 212.

6. Current developments of note include work on several ANSI standards, including Standard Order Forms (Z39.SC36), Serial Claim Form (Z39.SC42), Serial Holdings Statements at the Detailed Level (Z39.SC E), and the publication of *Serial Holdings Statements at the Summary Level* (Z39.42–1980); as well as the creation of an ALA/RTSD/SS Ad Hoc Committee on Union Lists of Serials, charged with publication of techniques and methods used in union listing in the ALA *Guidelines* series (see *RTSD Newsletter* 5/6 (November/December 1980): 62).

7. Variant practices in serials management are thoroughly documented in *Manually Maintained Serials Records: Report of the Ad Hoc Committee* ... (Chicago: American Library Association, 1976), available as ERIC document ED 125549.

8. For a model in planning the representation of serials in a machine-readable AACR2 catalog, see *Future of the General Library Catalogs, Phase IV Reports: Working Paper on Serials* (Berkeley: General Library, University of California, 1978).

9. Michael Gorman, "The *Anglo-American Cataloguing Rules*, Second Edition," *Library Resources and Technical Services* 22/3 (Summer 1978): 219.

10. *RTSD Newsletter* 6/1 (January/February 1981): 5–6, and 6/3 (May/June 1981): 33–34; and *Cataloging Service Bulletin* 11 (Winter 1981): 45–53.

11. *ISBD(S): International Standard Bibliographic Description for Serials*. (London: IFLA International Office for UBC, 1977).

12. Jean S. Decker, "Catalog 'Closings' and Serials," *Journal of Academic Librarianship* 5/5 (November 1979): 261–65.

13. The option of "freezing" the old catalog is not viable for serials as a whole, as long as the need to update holdings and edit bibliographic records remains a possibility. Closing the catalog by imprint date is unfeasible for the same reasons.

14. For example, Berkeley recommended following LC's lead in this regard and correct only the form of entry. See *Future of the Catalogs*, p. 3.

15. Discussions of the impact of various catalog options on serials may be found in: "Report of the Alternative Catalog Evaluation Committee, University of California, Davis," *Alternative Catalog Newsletter* 15 (August 1979); "Bibliographic Access in the University of Michigan Library. Part I: Report of the Working Group on Closing the Catalog," *Alternative Catalog Newsletter* 4/5 (August 1978); and *To Close or Not to Close: Desuperimposition and the Future of the Catalogs, Committee on Bibliographic Control*. Phase I. (Berkeley: General Library, University of California, 1975.)

16. Application of AACR2 rules for description of microforms results in discrepancies between records for a single title in multiple formats. Pending resolution of the problem, LC is continuing to apply AACR1 to the description of microforms reproducing previously-published serials. See *RTSD Newsletter* 6/1 (January/February 1981): 6–7.

17. Ann Turner, "The Effects of AACR2 on Serials Cataloging," *Serials Librarian* 4/2 (Winter 1979): 181.

18. The Linda Hall Library is in effect closing its book catalog with the third edition and plans to produce an all-AACR2 holdings list. See "Serials News," *Serials Librarian* 4/2 (Winter 1979): 256.

19. LC considered this for their check-in file (see *LC Information Bulletin* 39/8 (February 22, 1980): 63), but apparently had decided against it by January 1981.

20. Mina Daniels, "Future of the Card Catalog Committee: Preliminary Report Southern Illinois University at Carbondale," *Alternative Catalog Newsletter* 2 (June 1978): 39. For additional arguments supporting classification of serials in general, see Lynn S. Smith, "To Classify or Not to Classify," *Serials Librarian* 2/4 (Summer 1978): 371–85.

21. Decker, "Catalog 'Closings,' " p. 264.

22. Southern Illinois University, Report of Ad-hoc Serials Subcommittee of the Future of the Card Catalog Committee, January 30, 1980.

23. State University of New York at Buffalo. Report of Subcommittee on Continuing Titles of the Task Force on the Future of Bibliographic Access, December 8, 1980.

24. Lynn S. Smith. *A Practical Approach to Serials Cataloging* (Greenwich, CT: JAI Press, 1978).

25. Osborn, *Serial Publications*, p. 140.

26. Smith, *A Practical Approach*, p. 255–56.

27. *To Close or Not to Close*, p. 18.

28. Michael Gorman, "The Current State of Standardization in the Cataloging of Serials," *Library Resources and Technical Services* 19/4 (Fall 1975): 311.

29. C. Sumner Spalding, "*ISBD(S)* and Title Main Entry for Serials," *Drexel Library Quarterly* 11/3 (July 1975): 25.

30. Lois Mai Chan, "AACR 6 and the Corporate Mystique," *Library Resources and Technical Services* 21/1 (Winter 1977): 59.

31. The broader question of compatibility with CONSER records, while assuredly critical, is beyond the scope of this essay.

32. Osborn, *Serial Publications*, p. 213.

33. Ibid., p. 314.

34. Turner, "The Effects of AACR2," p. 213.

35. "Bibliographic Access," p. 16.

36. Huibert Paul, "Serials Processing: Manual Control vs. Automation," *Library Resources and Technical Services* 21/4 (Fall 1977): 345.

THE CENTRAL SERIAL RECORD AT NEW YORK PUBLIC LIBRARY: AN ANALYSIS AND A SURVEY*

Minna C. Saxe

In most, if not all, libraries, one part of the work is the compilation of statistics. It is necessary to ascertain how many books are ordered, how many reference questions are answered, and how many books circulate in a given period of time. Although such statistics are kept methodically, they are almost always selective in nature and never reflect the total operation or even any aspect of that operation in depth. In addition, within a particular library, departments may define items counted differently; this is certainly true among libraries! When counting how many books are ordered, what is actually counted — the number of titles, of volumes, or of both. And how are volumes counted if an order reads "for all volumes in print."

What also happens frequently, especially in this period of rapidly changing technology, is that library procedures change yet the statistical forms do not. Terms are sometimes redefined or an addendum is added to the original statistics form. But even though thought is given to changing statistics forms, it is often a low priority item.

Library statistics are usually compiled monthly and then are cumulated to form the basis for the library's annual report. So, in many libraries, statistics are the basis for much planning, which is therefore based on figures which do not adequately reflect the total and/or current procedures.

Another type of figures often needed by libraries is when a person or institution outside the library requests information in the form of a survey or a general statement. The library must interpolate the data collected for the monthly statistics or, more likely than not, make an educated estimation.

It is this author's opinion that the only way to obtain a basis for

---

*Material in this paper has been adapted from two reports which the author wrote when she was Serials Planning and Coordination Librarian at the Research Libraries of New York Public Library in 1980/81.

any reliable library figures is to analyze the procedure(s) and/or the product(s) as well as to inventory methodically the said product(s), be they the book ordering system and/or the shelf list. In addition to obtaining an authoritative set of figures, the investigator is able by analyzing the procedures in the library's operation, to offer suggestions for possible changes.

CSR and Serial Processing

As Serials Coordination and Planning Librarian at the Research Libraries of New York Public Library in 1980/81, I was asked to perform such tasks in regard to the institution's Central Serial Record (CSR). In order to perform a satisfactory inventory of CSR, it was necessary for me to analyze the procedures which were performed in the totality of serial processing. It was assumed that the CSR inventory would also provide the answer to questions about the libraries' serial holdings and that both the report on the procedures and suggestions for changes and the inventory would serve as a basis in possible conversion of the files to an automated data base.

To understand what exactly was involved in such a two-pronged investigation, it is necessary to know something about CSR and serial processing at New York Public Library. Serials (i.e., standing order items) are ordered by the Serial Ordering Section and received initially by the Serial Adding Section in the Acquisitions Division and are cataloged by the Serial Cataloging Section in the Catalogue Division. (Both divisions are part of the Preparation Services Department.) Therefore, individuals in three sections in two different divisions can and do make decisions concerning the processing of any specific serial title.

The Central Serial Record is a file of 976 drawers; it contains standard-sized library cards for all standing order items. These cards contain acquisition information on what is called the Serial Acquisition Record Card (or SAR Card); bibliographic information as provided by the Serial Cataloging Section on a Face Card; and holdings information on a Tabulated Card (Tab Card). Most serial titles contain at least one of each of these cards, filed with the Face Card(s) first, the SAR Card(s) next a   last, the Tab Card(s). All serial titles do not have a Face Card, a.. ₀AR Card, and a Tab Card. The processing of an item determines which cards are applicable (e.g., a standing order item, which is treated as a monographic series, has an SAR Card and a Tab Card but no Face Card). In addition, within each type of card, there can be several varieties. Therefore one item could have one form of Tab Card and another item could have another form.

CSR was established in Fall, 1966, when records which had been filed in several locations (e.g., Official Serial Catalogue, Official Documents Catalogue, and the Serial Acquisition File) were consolidated into one master file. The records were converted to CSR as new pieces were added for these records. Therefore, initially, CSR contained only active titles. A decision was later made, however, to include in CSR inactive titles and since May, 1978, many (but not all) inactive standing order titles are being systematically converted for and refiled into CSR.

When a record is converted for CSR, no changes are made to the physical cards. One of the results of this no-change policy is there are many divergent forms of entry for records in CSR. Whatever cataloging rules were in practice when the item was initially cataloged determines the choice and form of entry for the record. It should be noted that when an item ceases publication or changes title, for example, it is recataloged and at that time the item is cataloged using the current cataloging rules. Therefore, it is frequently necessary when looking for a record in CSR to try several forms of an entry as well as several choices of entry. (CSR is a main entry only file with few cross references.)

Finding information in CSR can also be hampered by the fact that not all hodlings are recorded on Tab Cards. The Research Libraries of New York Public Library differentiate between serials — which are called non-currents — and periodicals — which are called currents. Non-currents' pieces are added to Tab Cards as they are received by the Serial Adding Section; currents are not. Instead, currents are checked in on visible record files located in various locations in the Public Service Departments. The currents are entered onto the Tab Card only after they have been processed for binding or when the microform arrives. Needless to say, there can be delays of more than a year between the time a piece is checked in on a visible record file and the time it is prepared to go to the bindery.

The CSR is filed using rules which disregard almost all articles and prepositions (including those in the initial position as well as those used internally in a corporate name, title, or other entries). The current, *Journal of the History of Ideas* files as Journal History Ideas. Within a CSR record, the cards are filed sequentially for both Face Cards and Tab Cards but SAR Cards are filed in reverse order with the earliest card filed last.

The size of CSR as well as the above-mentioned complexities make CSR a difficult file to use and yet it is used heavily and used well. As the file is not a public one, the staffs of the Serial Ordering Section, the Serial Adding Section and the Serial Cataloging Section as well as many staff members from other sections in the Preparation Services Department and from the Public Services Department are constantly consulting CSR, both in person and by telephone.

Analysis of CSR

In the analysis of CSR, suggestions were made both to streamline serial operations and to provide better control of the data in CSR (whether or not these data are converted into an automated data base). Changes in CSR center on providing authority control, through a variety of proposed systems, all of which call for the use of cross references and see also references. It was also recommended that the extensive information that is currently listed on Tab Cards be consolidated to eliminate cards; in addition, with much outdated acquisitions information listed on multiple SAR Cards, these cards could be removed from CSR, while retaining only one SAR card per order.

The most important aspect of maintaining a truly Central Serial Record is to establish a Serial Division which will monitor all aspects of serial work; a unified division can provide the necessary management to implement changes in procedures and in CSR itself.

CSR Survey

Monthly statistics have always been kept for all aspects of serial processing (including those procedures directly related to CSR); these statistics, however, are typical of most library statistics discussed above.

After analyzing CSR and listing suggestions for possible changes it was necessary to know accurately how many cards are in CSR and what these cards represent. It was therefore agreed upon to do an inventory of CSR which would also provide the Research Libraries of New York Public Library with a basis in determining their serial holdings.

Conducting such an inventory turned out to be a very time-consuming task. The first step was to determine the total population to be surveyed, in this case, the total number of cards, records and unique entries in CSR. (Card was defined as any 3-inch by 5-inch piece of paper, whether it be library stock card or mulitple-order slip; each record represented one order, and each unique entry, a bibliographic entity. To exemplify, *Journal of the History of Ideas* is a current title for which CSR lists two subscriptions; it is one unique entry and two records.) Since it would be impossible to count every card, record, and unique entry in SCR, an accepted surveying practice, which is to select drawers randomly and to count every card, record, and unique entry in those drawers was employed. Consuling a table of 5,000 random digits (such a table is available in the appendix of most books on statistics), it was decided to use the first three digits of the five digit numbers in the first ten lines. For example, if the first line (line number 0) reads 45678, then the cards, etc. in drawer 456 were counted; this procedure was followed for line number zero through nine.

In each of the ten drawers, the following steps were taken:

(1) The cards were compressed and measured with a ruler. Using the standard of 90 cards per inch, the total number of cards per drawer was determined.

(2) The guide cards were counted.

(3) A card-by-card count was taken to determine the number of unique bibliographic entries and records.

A table was constructed which contained seven columns running across the page: Drawer Number, Inclusive Letters, Number of Inches, Number of Cards, Number of Guide Cards, Number of Unique Entries and Number of Records. Eleven lines ran down the side of the page: Lines one through ten respond to lines zero through nine of the first three digits of the randomly selected digits table. Line ten contains the total number of inches, cards, and other material in the randomly selected ten drawers. Using the data from this table, a second table was developed which provided the number of inches, cards, and so on for the ten-drawer span and also the ten-drawer average. A third table was designed to show the total number of inches, cards, and other material for the 976 drawers. These figures were obtained by multiplying the averages in the preceding table by 976. In addition, the following ratios were calculated: the number of cards per unique entry, the number of cards per record, and the number of records per unique entry.

The second step, and probably the important one in a survey of this type was the survey design. Initially, a list of 15 questions was compiled; these questions were involved with areas not covered by the monthly statistics compiled by any of the sections dealing with CSR. Such information as how many main entries in CSR are titles and how many are corporate bodies was one such question.

From these questions came a preliminary survey draft, in which each survey form represented one unique bibliographic entry in CSR. The survey format then went through several major design changes; with each change, the survey grew in size from less than one page to three pages (it had been assumed that the opposite would occur — that the survey would be consolidated and therefore shorter with each draft). Many of the changes were made for formatting reasons, such as the reordering of categories, the introduction of alphabetic and numeric designations (which was later changed to numeric designations only), the devising of mutually exclusive categories and the combining of categories into broader areas. The final draft, which is Figure 1, was so designed that the collected data could be key-punched onto data cards. (Although the key-punching was not done, the survey format was found most expedient for detailed manual analyses.)

By a process of testing each draft, not only was the format rearranged but also the survey's contents changed. In some cases, categories were removed when it was found that they might be difficult to answer and/or might not produce any meaningful data. In the main, however, categories were added or expanded to obtain data not asked for in earlier drafts. Instructions for completing the survey together with a list of definitions of terms used in the survey were compiled and altered during the testing period. The final version of the survey form was reached by designing, discussing, testing and redesigning until all the necessary changes were made both in format and in content.

The third step was to determine who was to complete the survey and how many items of the total population were to be surveyed. Throughout the extensive testing period it had become obvious that as the survey grew in length and complexity it was necessary to have a limited number of people filling out the survey forms and that those individuals be ones who had worked on the survey design and had tested it in its several drafts. Three such individuals (including this author) were selected; each participant filled out a survey form for the same five unique entries. The completed forms were discussed and minor differences were reconciled. It was agreed that by this stage the three participants were totally conversant with the survey form, the definitions and the instructions.

It was difficult to determine how many surveys it was necessary to complete in order to provide a valid sampling. The literature consulted on this matter provided little information but to reaffirm that "small samples are often the *least* of the errors present." The decision was made to complete 250 survey forms. Preliminary analysis would then be made and if the data appeared valid, then no more surveys would be completed. If the data were not valid, then 250 more surveys would be completed.

In order to select the items to be surveyed, again a table of random units was used. The method devised was to use the last three digits of the five digit unit as the drawer to be selected and the first two digits as the number of inches to be measured in from the front of the drawer, which is called on the survey form "the address." In cases where the last three digits were greater than 976 (the number of drawers), the random unit was omitted. If the first two digits were greater than 13 (the number of inches of the longest drawer measured), then the first digit was eliminated and the second digit was designated as the address. Using such a system it was surprising to discover that in a sampling of this size, two survey forms were duplicates.

The completion of the survey forms caused no major problems. Due to the length of the survey and the complexity of CSR, each form took a minimum of ten minutes to complete.

Although designed otherwise, the survey forms were all tabulated manually. It was possible and indeed fortunate to batch the survey forms and tabulate the data in several groups. By employing this method, it became evident that the statistical percentages remained constant, regardless of the number of surveys tabulated. It was therefore decided that it was not necessary to complete any more than the decided upon 250 surveys. The tabulations were completed by collating the surveys by category and then listing the results in three columns: number of surveys, percentage of surveys and number of unique entries.

Conclusion

Using the methodology and techniques described above, the author was able to analyze both the procedures surrounding CSR and CSR, per se, as well as to conduct an inventory of CSR. The two reports which were prepared to describe in detail both the procedures and the results of this investigation are to be used both to provide the library with information on its current serial situation as well as to plan for future changes. These reports provide necessary data, which can never be obtained through the customary procedure of compiling statistics.

No. _____

FIGURE 1

NEW YORK PUBLIC LIBRARY, RESEARCH LIBRARIES

Central Serial Record Survey

Location
    Drawer _____ Address _____

Count

0.10	Number of Records _____					
0.20	Number of Cards and Slips _____					
	Record	1	2	3	4	5
0.21	Number of Face Cards					
0.22	Number of S.A.R. Cards					
0.23	Number of Tab Cards					
0.24	Slip Only					

Type of Record (Card)

1.10	Current		
1.11	Temp. Cat. _____	☐	1.11
1.12	Full Cat. _____	☐	1.12
1.13	Uncataloged _____	☐	1.13
1.20	Non-Current		
1.21	Book Continuation		
1.21.1	Complete _____	☐	1.21.1
1.21.2	Incomplete _____	☐	1.21.2
1.21.3	Unknown _____	☐	1.21.3
1.22	Monographic Series		
1.22.1	Anal. Scattered _____	☐	1.22.1
1.22.2	Anal. Kept Together _____	☐	1.22.2
1.22.3	N.S.C.M. _____	☐	1.22.3
1.22.4	Sep. _____	☐	1.22.4
1.22.5	S.I.D. _____	☐	1.22.5
1.23	Non-Monographic Serial _____	☐	1.23
1.30	Newspaper _____	☐	1.30

N.Y.P.L. – C.S.R. Survey   No._____

        1.40   Other
        1.41   Metro_____ ☐ 1.41
        1.42   Cross-Reference_____ ☐ 1.42
        1.43   Membership Card_____ ☐ 1.43
        1.44   Discard_____ ☐ 1.44
        1.45   Specify_____ 1.45

Indexed
        2.10   Indexed_____ ☐ 2.10

Cancellation
        3.10   Cancellation_____ ☐ 3.10

Type of Record (Slip)
        4.10   Purchase Order_____ ☐ 4.10
        4.20   Exchange Request_____ ☐ 4.20
        4.30   Sample Request_____ ☐ 4.30
        4.40   Beg Request_____ ☐ 4.40

        5.10   Claim_____ ☐ 5.10

        6.10   Replacement_____ ☐ 6.10

Bibliographic Information
        7.10   Main Entry
        7.11   Personal Name_____ ☐ 7.11
        7.12   Corporate Name
        7.12.1   N.Y.P.L. Inverted Form__ ☐ 7.12.1
        7.12.2   Other_____ ☐ 7.12.2
        7.13   Conference Name_____ ☐ 7.13
        7.14   Title_____ ☐ 7.14

        8.10   Classmark
        8.11   Billings_____ ☐ 8.11
        8.12   Billings w/Discrete No.__ ☐ 8.12
        8.13   Fixed Order_____ ☐ 8.13
        8.14   More than one Classmark_ ☐ 8.14

        9.10   Closed Entry
        9.11   Continued Note_____ ☐ 9.11
        9.12   No Continued Note____ ☐ 9.12
        9.20   Open Entry
        9.21   Active_____ ☐ 9.21
        9.22   Inactive_____ ☐ 9.22

N.Y.P.L. — CSR Survey   No._____

10.10	Country of Publication	
10.11	U.S.A._____ ☐	10.11
10.12	Specify_____	10.12
11.10	Document	
11.11	U.S. Federal_____ ☐	11.11
11.12	Other_____ ☐	11.12

Acquisitions Information

12.10	Division	
12.11	G.R.&H._____ ☐	12.11
12.12	Econ. & Pub. Affairs_____ ☐	12.12
12.13	Sci. & Tech._____ ☐	12.13
12.14	Specify_____	12.14
13.10	Membership_____ ☐	13.10
13.20	Exchange_____ ☐	13.20
13.30	Gift	
13.31	P.A.I.S._____ ☐	13.31
13.32	N.T.B._____ ☐	13.32
13.33	Specify_____	13.33
13.40	PL–480_____ ☐	13.40
14.10	Direct	
14.11	Publisher_____ ☐	14.11
14.12	Microform Producer____ ☐	14.12
14.20	Dealer	
14.21	Faxon_____ ☐	14.21
14.22	Ebsco_____ ☐	14.22
14.23	Nijhoff_____ ☐	14.23
14.24	Harrassowitz_____ ☐	14.24
14.25	Stevens & Brown_____ ☐	14.25
14.26	Specify_____ ☐	14.26
14.30	Depository Item_____ ☐	14.30
15.10	Special Fund_____ ☐	15.10

Physical Format

16.10	Form of Receipt	
16.11	Paper_____ ☐	16.11
16.12	Microform_____ ☐	16.12

N.Y.P.L. – CSR Survey   No._____

      17.10   Back File
      17.11   Bound_____ ☐ 17.11
      17.12   Microform
      17.12.1   Commercially Produced __☐ 17.12.1
      17.12.2   Produced In-House_____☐ 17.12.2
      17.13   No Back File Kept_____☐ 17.13
      17.14   Decision Not Made_____☐ 17.14
      17.15   Physical Status Unknown_☐ 17.15

Source of Information
      18.10   Face Card
      18.11   O.S._____☐ 18.11
      18.12   O.D._____☐ 18.12
      18.13   1966–71_____☐ 18.13
      18.14   S.A.D.P.O._____☐ 18.14
      18.15   Other_____☐ 18.15

      19.10   Temp. or Dummy_____☐ 19.10
                         S.A.R. Card

Xerox top face card. If no face card xerox top S.A.R. card.

                                                             Date:_____/81
                                                             Initials:_____

March 1981

SERIALS AUTOMATION:
FOUR YEARS LATER

John Riddick

Central Michigan University's Park Library holds a distinctive leadership position in the application and development of the OCLC Serials Control Subsystem. As one of the earliest and one of the few major university libraries to totally convert from a manual to an automated serials system, the Park Library's experiences form a worthy case study of its development. This examination springs from the initial report of the system's installation by Nancy Melin as published in the Fall, 1978, issue of *The Serials Librarian*.

After four years of continued use and development, the Park Library remains enthusiastically committed to the application and advancement of the OCLC Serials Control Subsystem. Despite the results of a recent study indicating the greater per-issue check in cost, the system's public service use has taken quantum leaps bounding over the objections of manual system supporters. The replacement of a shabby set of manual records by the increasingly refined serials local data record has established a finer technical support base to the serials operations. Hence strengthened public services, centralized accurate technical records and the prospect of future claiming and binding enhancements map the past and lay claim to the future.

Following the two-year endeavor to bring the periodical collection on-line, a terminal was placed in the Reference Department for staff and patron use. Once the public service staff had gained an interpretive familiarity with the local data record, its use exploded from 2,943 searches in July, 1979, to 5,158 by July, 1980. The subsequent demand for a second terminal was predictable and indeed met with its installation in September, 1980. It is conceivable that increasing patron demand for terminal access and the continued planned obsolescence of a public manual title/location file will spur the installation of two or three additional terminals. The forestalling force to complete reliance of system-supplied serials information is the lack of OCLC Sunday hours during which the Park Library serves 13 percent of its total patrons.

Hand in hand with the increased public use of the Serials Control

Subsystem came numerous technical developments by the serials department of the local data record which furthered greater use and confidence in the system's value. Initially in the claims field and now temporarily in a separate remarks field, a series of fixed statements were developed to specify various types of claiming actions which supported public service needs and were, of course, integral to the claiming operations. Example statements included: "Cl.f. v 13 p 3 811115," "Reclaimed 811215," and "Cl.f. v 13 p 3, direct, 811115." The first two notations related to "due" claims placed with the vendor or publisher as expressed in the fund field. The latter claim represented one for a vendor held title but was sent, however, directly to the publisher. Claims for duplicate issues, sample issues, invoices, and replacement issues are presently handled outside the automated system and would not look to be easily integrated into the proposed claiming component.

Local enhancements to the binding field similarly aided the work of the public service staff. As an aid in the location of specific holdings in the binding process, two notes were developed. The first alerted public services that the volume was incomplete and being held in the bindery, but available for patron use. It emerged as "h v 1 p 1–3, 5–6 (1979)." The second note indicated the absence of the serial volume from the local library at the commercial bindery. It became "b v 15 p 7–12 (1980) d 810104--810204" thus indicating when the volume had left the library and when it would return. Hence without frustrating referral and without guessing or surmising, the public service staff found growing patron satisfaction in the specific information supplied even if it represented bad news.

Two small developments in the local data record further assisted public service work. Formerly the receipt of duplicate issues was recorded in the remarks field. This became confusing as public service staff began to look for them if the original issue was not available. Departmental staff shortages precluded intensive organization, rapid retrieval and responsive solution of their origin. The consequent cluttering of the remarks field complicated public service interpretation. The removal of duplicate issues from the local data record and their release to the stacks solved at least the public service portion of the problem.

A second change involved the expression of holdings for mixed microform formats. Although the local data record indicated call numbers for both formats, the holdings statement indicated the holdings for only the format supported by a standing order subscription. By the inclusion of the holdings for both micro formats e.g., "Microfiche v 11–15 (1976–1981)//Microfilm v 1–10 (1966–1975)," the patron could be provided the specific format related call number for the volume desired.

In general the public service needs for development or modification of the serials local data record have been logical and resolved within the limitations of time and money. Two questions, however, continue to demand attention in addition to Sunday availability of the system. First, the continued pressure for maximizing system response time is vital. The frustration for staff and patron alike is sometimes unbearable as both have turned away from the terminal to seek less likely means of resolution.

Second, for whom is the local data record constructed? As the record has developed at the Park Library, there have been valid technical service needs for adding information to it. This is, however, counterproductive to the ease of interpretation by the patron and public service staff. Furthermore it frequently results in a two-screen record which again relates to system response time. Accordingly, as a member of the OCLC Serials Control Subsystem Advisory Group, I have asked for a feasibility study for the development of a single public service screen made up of selected data from the entire record as a means of easing public use.

Certain changes and developments of the local data record have occurred in response to specific operational requirements of the serials department. A recent need has been the greater development of information in the fund field. In lieu of the claiming component, the expression of source — either vendor's name or "direct" in case of a publisher — along with vendor title number, and purchase order number has been necessary to facilitate claims handling. For local needs a fund code has also been inserted in this field. Thus a typical expression would appear as: "660–BUS; Faxon (061324) p.o. 01376s." The proposed claiming component will eliminate the fund field, but it seems to make adequate provisions for this data.

The development of the binding field for public service support has already been discussed. Additional changes for technical needs included the construction of a bindery definition or pickup schedule especially for titles with a monthly or more frequent publishing schedule. A recent decision to include buckram color and color number to the field will aid current processing and envision its expression in a future binding component.

As the development of the local data record occurred at the Park Library, the expression of missing volumes in the retrospective holdings field became confused. Was it to mean those holdings which were never in the collection, or those which were once present but now missing? A current inventory of the retrospective or bound holdings will result in the positive statement of what is in the library. Any volumes shown to be missing by the inventory will be expressed as missing. A typical holdings statement could thus read, "v 10–21, 23–30 (1960–1971, 1973–1980)//Missing v 22 (1972)." This would mean volume 22 was found to be missing in inventory and volumes 1–9 would be understood to be *desiderium*.

Since 1976 the number of OCLC enhancements to the Serials Control Subsystems have been small in number. Perhaps the greatest improvement came in automatic check in which the development of the "R" or received command, update and send. The efficiencies gained here were immediately apparent. The change allowing for the retrieval of the bibliographic record and the holding libraries directly from the serials system has been helpful. The added qualifiers to the existing search keys have supported bibliographic searching conducted by serials acquisitions. The Park Library was extremely appreciative of OCLC's transfer rather than elimination of the data contained in the claims field as they prepare to bring up the claims component. It would appear that the claiming component and many addition enhancements are not far away and their addition will greatly improve automated serials operations.

Let's turn then and examine the future possibilities of the OCLC Serials Control Subsystem for the Park Library four years in the future. Realizing that in all likelihood the Serials Control Subsystem cannot be financially rationalized against technical services cost savings, it must, therefore, be supportive of unquantified intelligence costs of public service. For a university library this must mean system availability on Sunday. Response time must be shortened. Screen displays designed with the patron in mind such as the aforementioned serial local data record and possible help screens should be considered.

For technical services the installation of the claiming and binding components are mandatory and seem to be coming. The development of automated means for controlling pocket parts, updating pages, and special revisions of legal publications are needed. Attention needs to be paid to the nagging problem of the manual intervention required to change the next expected date when the frequency status is coded U, Z, or left blank. The Park Library must better define its standards for what information will be retained on the local data record for a cancelled or ceased title. The construction of links from serials to the acquisition system and name-address file will be vital for effective claiming, acquisition, invoice payment, and fund management operations.

The execution of even a few of these concepts would mean an increasingly responsive and meaningful basis for providing excellence in the public and technical service to the teaching and research needs of Central Michigan University.

POPULAR SERIALS

Michael H. Randall

Popular serials in libraries present special opportunities and problems in relation to various aspects of the selection, processing and use of library materials. These special aspects will be discussed here.

For the purpose of this discussion, popular serials can most readily be defined by what they are not: they are not the serials that librarians usually select for their reference and research value; they are not even the mass circulation periodicals covered by the standard indexing services that are used in most libraries.

For the most part popular serials are aimed more at audiences that are interested in entertainment or information on leisure activities than for those who are looking for serious or scholarly treatment of a topic. They are, usually, consumer magazines that emanate from commercial publishers. These magazines are profit-making operations in which most of the profit comes from advertising revenues.

The popular serials discussed here are publications that many librarians have eschewed for their libraries. If librarians are, in fact, aware of them, it is not because these publications are included in their libraries' collections, but because they see them on magazine racks and newsstands. Included in this group are the legions of mass-circulation magazines that cover such topics as mass-media entertainment, recreation, sports, personalities, adventure, sex, romance and humor.

Selection

The selection of serial publications for library collections is a serious matter. A decision to initiate a serial subscription implies not only an indefinite commitment to fund an ever-increasing subscription cost, but it also commits processing costs. If the title is retained permanently, growing amounts of space for housing will be required as well as budgets to support binding or retention in microformat. In view of costs alone, the selection of serials for libraries must be a carefully considered matter. And this is to say nothing of the consideration that the librarian must choose from a vast body of more serials than any single library can acquire.

To these factors must be added the realization that the changing nature of serial publications obviates any single absolutely reliable means of evaluating titles for selection. Popular magazines are especially subject to editorial change through the influence of the changing external conditions of public demand and perceived market characteristics.

Nevertheless, there are several methods or aids that librarians responsible for collection development have used to identify magazines for their libraries. One method, by far the most common, is to include in library collections those periodicals that are covered by the index and abstract services to which the library subscribes. Another method is to rely on reviews and standard listings of titles. This inludes lists and reviews aimed at libraries, as well as reviews and listings for practitioners and scholars in particular disciplines and subjects. Yet another method, employed for journal selection, is to use citation analyses to attempt to identify those publications which appear to have the greatest influence on scholarly research and study.

These three methods all have their advantages. Their use almost surely guarantees that the librarian can develop a core collection of publications that are commonly agreed to be essential for conventional reference, research and information needs. Use of these methods for selection of serials will result in a collection that is virtually identical with the collections of other libraries of the same type and size. The inherent disadvantage of these three methods is that they are insufficient by themselves, even though many librarians employ one or more of these methods exclusive of any other means of selection. In effect, by doing this the librarian abdicates responsibility for collection development by relying only on others to say what shall be in the collection.

Specific disadvantages of using only these three methods are: (1) the published sources employed may be out of date (in fact any published source which lists or reviews serials runs the danger of obsolescence, in view of the changing nature of serials); (2) a particular review, list, or choice of titles for indexing or abstracting only represents the opinion of an individual or a particular group; (3) the orientation of the source used for selection may not coincide with the library's orientation; (4) citation analyses are limited only to measuring the preferences of the community of individuals who have written and published results of their research.[1]

And so, although these methods of aiding in serials selection have their advantages, they are insufficient by themselves. What is necessary is for the librarian to relate the collection to the community served by the library. Much of this can be accomplished by use of the aforementioned sources in selection, but their limitations make additional means necessary. The librarian must be in touch with the preferences of the community served, including both the actual users of the library and the potential users. The benefits of taking this approach are that it relates directly to the needs of the users (and thus to the goals and objectives of the library) and that it reflects current interests and trends. Librarians should realize that this approach requires active solicitation or surveying of the preferences and interests of the library's users as well as the nonusers. Opinions received may be subjective, inconsistent and uninformed, and community interests and preferences may not coincide with the goals of the library.[2]

When user demand coincides with the perceived goals of the library, everyone is happy. In such cases magazine selection satisfies community tastes as well as librarians' perceptions of the ideal means to serve.

But when popular taste does not coincide with librarians' conceptions of quality, then libraries fail to serve. Bill Katz has discussed this matter:

> Libraries have to give up the traditional emphasis on quality and adopt a more realistic selection policy based on relevance — relevance not only of the magazine *per se*, but relevance of the magazine to the community it serves. If one subscribes to the notion that good, better and best are only relative, if the library is for every man, why should it not be just as much for the housewife or for the working girl who enjoys *True Story* as much as for the better educated suburban matron who gets a similar treat from *McCall's* or *Ladies' Home Journal*?[3]

The library collection should include magazines which appeal to all segments of the community, and not merely to the well-read portion with which the librarian identifies most closely. While many libraries provide *Esquire*, how many provide *Saga*? Almost every library has *Time* and *Newsweek*, but how many have *National Enquirer*? If a library has *Sports Illustrated*, should it also be able to provide the *Daily Racing Form*?

One reason for selecting popular magazines for library collections is that these titles attract to the library people in the community who would otherwise not go to the library. Once in the library these new users may avail themselves of other library services. Another reason that librarians should select popular periodicals for libraries is that more people read periodicals for entertainment than for information or practical purposes. Concerning this Katz says:

> ... while no more than 10 to 20 percent of Americans read

book, at least 80 to 90 percent read magazines. If the library is concerned with reading *per se*, more attention might be given to the attraction of *True Story* and the *Reader's Digest* as compared to the average book. Put another way, the average reader is more interested in fun than intellectual pursuits.[4]

Another reason to select popular serials for library collections is for reference and research value. Certain popular periodicals may be of permanent value in connection with particular disciplines or fields of interest. For example, files of the most popular (in terms of total circulation) of popular American magazines, *TV Guide*, are retained permanently by libraries supporting programs of education and research in the field of television. Another reason for retaining popular serials in a library is to support study and research in popular culture.

Obviously, a library cannot stock and retain every serial that any user or potential user may conceivably request, but the library should be able to satisfy all major areas of demand for reading and information in the community served. Further, the library should strive, through its serials selection, never to be dismissed as inadequate by any group in the community because it cannot meet their demands.

Acquisition

A library may not always find it possible, or desirable, to acquire popular serials through conventional mail and subscription arrangements. In some cases, especially for titles sold only at retail outlets, or for titles, such as those associated with a particular sport, which are sold seasonally, the only practical approach may be for a library staff member to purchase each copy separately, out of a petty cash fund or through a reimbursement system. This approach may also be necessary treatment for some titles in libraries which are situated within large organizations, where mail goes through many hands. In such environments, issues of certain extremely popular magazines, covers temptingly visible to one and all as they pass through the mail handling operation, sometimes never reach their intended destinations. Another approach to this problem is to have the magazine mailed to a library staff member's home or to a special post office box. This latter approach may also be an effective means of speeding up receipt for issues of titles with timely editorial matter.

Retention

When a library acquires a popular magazine to satisfy readers' demands for current issues, the library may choose to retain only issues covering a specified time period, such as one year, for example. Disposal of older issues can be carried out on a "rolling" basis, with the oldest issue discarded at the same time that a new issue is shelved, or it can be done as a project carried out at an annual or other frequency basis. For extremely popular titles attrition through heavy use, mutilation and theft may effectively take care of the disposal problem.

In cases in which it is desirable to retain files of a popular serial title, the library must choose an appropriate medium for retention. If it is decided to bind the title, it should be remembered that one of the special problems associated with the binding of issues of popular serials is the effect that high levels of use of current issues have on binding for permanent retention. When high use results in worn, mutilated and missing issues of a popular magazine, the library staff must choose between attempting to get replacement issues (often a futile gesture) or binding an incomplete volume. If this problem is chronic for a particular popular title, the library would do well to subscribe to an additional copy for the purpose of binding, or to arrange with a commercial binder to receive prebound volumes of the magazine.

Although binding is the traditional method of permanent retention for serial publications in many libraries, the librarian should consider microform retention as an alternative. Many popular periodicals are available in microfilm and microfiche editions from commercial micropublishers. In view of the prolific nature and poor paper quality of many of these magazines, retention in microformat offers decided advantages in terms of preservation and space savings.

Cataloging

Cataloging is a means of organizing and an aid to retrieving a library's serial holdings. If a library does not permanently retain periodicals, there is no need to catalog them, so long as this policy poses no problems for the users and the staff. Usually, libraries that do not retain their periodicals permanently do not have large collections of serials, so there are no problems of access or retrieval.

A library that retains periodical titles permanently should catalog these titles in order to integrate them into the collection and make them accessible. When some titles are retained permanently and others, such as popular periodicals, are not, these latter titles should also be cataloged or otherwise included in the same files as the permanent titles. If this is not done, these titles may be overlooked by users and staff.

Location

Current issues of popular periodicals should be shelved with other periodicals in the library's collection to accommodate browsing, although there are reasons, discussed below, for separating them. Ideally a library should shelve the latest issue of all of its periodicals on display units that show off the latest issue and also provide space for recent back issues of each title. In many libraries there is not enough space for this sort of arrangement, and current periodicals may be shelved flat on regular book shelves. This arrangement may be used exclusively, or the collection of current periodicals may be divided between flat and display shelving. As a comparison of the storage capabilities of the two types of arrangement, Keyes Metcalf calculated that display shelving provides space for one and one-half to two titles per square foot of library floor space, while flat shelving can accommodate up to five titles per square foot.[5]

Although the best arrangement for shelving current issues of popular periodicals is to place them with other periodicals in order to encourage use of as many titles as possible, certain factors may prevent this arrangement. If a library is divided into subject departments containing both books and periodicals, popular periodicals may not fit comfortably into any of the departments. One alternative is to arbitrarily assign the popular titles to a single department. A more attractive approach might be to locate these titles in or near a lobby or casual relaxing area as an encouragement to light or recreational reading.

Another factor that might call for separate shelving of some popular periodicals is the level of use. Some popular titles may be so much in demand that their use must be controlled. This is accomplished by locating them at or behind a public service desk and handing them out to users in response to requests. Unfortunately, such treatment may cut down on the use of a title. On the other hand, it may increase use by making the title available to more users over a longer period of time.

NOTES

1. David L. Perkins, ed., *Guidelines for Collection Development* (Chicago: American Library Association, 1979), p13–17.

2. Ibid.

3. William A. Katz, "Serials Selection," in Walter C. Allen, ed., *Serial Publications in Large Libraries* (Urbana: University of Illinois Graduate School of Library Science, 1970), p14.

4. Ibid., p13.

5. Keyes D. Metcalf, *Planning Academic and Research Library Buildings* (New York: McGraw-Hill, 1965), p107.

MANAGING AND BUILDING A NEWSPAPER COLLECTION

Linda Ervin

Newspapers have always been considered a nuisance amongst serials librarians. They are awkward to shelve, they are published on poor quality paper which deteriorates rapidly, and they are messy to use. Moreover, newspapers are difficult to access, since very few of them are indexed, and even when their bulk is reduced to microfilm, user resistance is heightened due in general to poorly designed equipment and lack of good quality machinery for hard copy reproduction.

Further, librarians and patrons alike tend to be infected by journalism's maxim that there is nothing more stale than yesterday's news. Since the bottom line of collection development and selection efforts has to be the usefulness, either present or future, of the material acquired, especially in these times of inflation and budget restraints, the question must be asked regarding the purpose of collecting organizing, maintaining and providing access to newspapers.

Any librarians who have been bitten by the bug of reference work which requires the use of newspapers will find it easy to refute these claims and, indeed, will argue that the products of research and scholarship in various disciplines would suffer irretrievably without the primary source material which is found in newspapers. Whether a drama critic needs access to reviews of Sarah Bernhardt's performances when she toured North America, or whether a lawyer has to investigate claims of false advertising in order to prepare for litigation, newspapers can provide the required information.

Genealogists can also attest to the fact that the missing links in their family trees can often be supplied through the birth, marriage and death announcements in newspapers. For the social historian studying Scandinavian immigration to Minnesota or the political scientist considering contemporary reaction to Premier Krushchev's "secret speech" to the XX Party Congress of the Communist Party of the Soviet Union, newspapers will be invaluable primary sources. Even for the casual user, the fascination of "old" newspapers is undeniable.

This essay, therefore, will focus on the basics of building a newspaper collection (selection tools and acquisition techniques) organizing the collection, preserving and conserving original paper copies as well as the pros and cons of microfilm and how to select newspapers on microfilm, and finally, how to provide access to newspapers through reference services. The effects of automation will also be discussed, particularly the trend towards full-text newspapers online, and the production of newspaper indexes in machine-readable format.

Definition

Although newspapers have usually been thought of by librarians as just another type of serial publication, they have little in common with other serials except for the fact that they are published at more or less regular intervals and are expected to continue publication indefinitely. Even though the process of separating newspapers from other types of serials can become a hair-splitting exercise, it can be useful because newspapers pose different problems in terms of acquiring, organizing, maintaining and accessing them.

The most logical definition focuses on a newspaper's content. It is generally aimed at a wide audience and reports current events within fairly short intervals of time (often daily, or semi-weekly or weekly). Newspapers usually contain advertisements, editorials, birth and death announcements and are normally printed on newsprint without a cover. There can be religious newspapers, or financial newspapers, or labor newspapers, but the tendency is to avoid classification of a serial publication as a newspaper if it emphasizes news of interest to a particular segment of society or which concentrates on one subject.

Building the Collection

Given that newspapers are an important addition to a library's collection, and having established the basic parameters within which newspapers are defined, it is then important to decide on the scope of the collection and finally to identify specific titles to acquire. The conventional wisdom dictates that newspapers are important in the context of their place of publication and their time frame along the historical continuum. The notable exceptions are, of course, the so-called "great" newspapers, like *The New York Times* and *Le Monde* (Paris, France), which are read for their international scope and the quality of their news analyses, not necessarily because they are published in New York and Paris respectively.

Thus, a library may decide to collect its local newspapers along with a cross-section of major national and international newspapers, but this decision really depends on the type of library and the user audience. A public library may want to emphasize local newspapers for its local history room and will purchase not only currently published newspapers but will seek out, through second hand book dealers and auctions or commercial micropublishers, those newspapers which date back to an earlier era in the city's history.

Academic and research libraries may be more interested in collecting newspapers to support area studies programs (for example, Mexican and Spanish newspapers for an Hispanic Studies program) or to provide grist for the mill of historical research. Special libraries may focus specifically on newspapers which tend to emphasize their particular subject areas (for example, the *Wall Street Journal* for a business library) or they may even want to subscribe to a commercial clippings service which can scan a variety of newspapers and provide them with only those articles relating to their area of concern.

Libraries will also have to consider whether they want to collect current or retrospective issues or both. They must also determine whether or not they will replace paper copy when the microfilm becomes available.

In selecting original newspapers, there are a number of national newspaper directories which can provide librarians with basic ordering information (title, place of publication, publisher's address, frequency, price, circulation and so on). *Ayer's Directory of Publications* covers the United States, and to a lesser extent, Canada and the Caribbean, while *Canadian Advertising Rates and Data* (Toronto: Maclean-Hunter) is a more comprehensive guide to currently published newspapers in Canada. For the U.K. and the international press, the *Newspaper Press Directory* (London) is a good source of information, and the *Annuaire de la presse francaise* provides details for the acquisition of French newspapers. Since the Library of Congress has such a broadly based newspaper collection, its *List of Currently Received Newspapers* is an important source of identification for newspaper titles. Unfortunately it does not provide needed ordering information.

In many cities, there is more than one newspaper published, and since most libraries cannot afford to subscribe to many newspapers, the selection librarian could choose according to circulation figures, to the longevity of the newspaper, or to the reputation of the newspaper. However, political affiliation could be an important element to consider, especially when selecting earlier newspapers. Although contemporary newspapers are undoubtedly biased, no matter whether their editorial stance is taken as "independent" or not, they are quite timely compared with 19th and early to mid-20th century journalistic efforts. Many would be considered libellous according to today's standards. Depending upon how specialized the collection is intended to be, the librarian may want to have both points of view represented, or may even be faced with cities where six daily newspapers were published in the days before the electronic media. For example, in the 1890s, Toronto boasted newspapers such as the *Globe*, the *Empire*, the *Mail*, the *World* and the *Leader*. In this case, the choice becomes difficult, the selector may have to simply resort to the criteria mentioned above.

Language of publication is also a factor in selection. Unless one is buying for a very specialized user (for example, students in German studies or Italian immigrants to the United States), the librarian will want to select a newspaper which most users can read. For example, an American library may be most interested in an English language newspaper from Calcutta, India and a library in Montreal may prefer a French-language newspaper from Beirut, Lebanon.

Since subscription costs for serials have spiralled and library budgets have seemingly dropped by a corresponding rate, libraries must look towards collection rationalization more seriously than ever before. It is always a good idea to consult union lists and library catalogues before deciding to place newspaper subscriptions, and then to decide whether patron needs could be met through interlibrary loans. Union lists such as the Library of Congress' *Newspapers in Microform, 1948--1972* (Washington: 1973) and its supplements, as well as the *Union List of Canadian Newspapers Held by Canadian Libraries* (Ottawa: National Library of Canada, 1977) are examples of reference sources which could prove very valuable for decisions made by selectors. Many other national libraries have published lists of library holdings of their countries' newspapers, and many individual compilers have produced regional lists.

In deciding whether or not interlibrary loans can satisfy user needs, it is important to consider whether the potential lending library charges for loans, and whether the library places a limit on the number of microfilm reels per order. For example, one major East Coast university library charges $5.00 per interlibrary loan request, and limits each loan to one reel at a time. It is only one of many libraries with this type of loan policy. Moreover, librarians must also realize that if a library holds a newspaper in original format only, it is highly unlikely that it will be available for interlibrary loan.

The question of whether to acquire and keep newspapers in either original or microform is a controversial one and cannot easily be resolved. With regard to a retrospective newspaper collection, unless a library has inherited one or has been in existence long enough to have collected newspapers for some time, the question may remain academic, since it is likely that only microforms will be available. However, if a library is just beginning to collect newspapers which happen to be published currently, the whole problem must be addressed, and must be incorporated into any collection development policy.

If newspapers are intended for current use only, then a library must order the paper copy, since obviously, it is going to arrive much faster than the microfilm version. However, if for example an American library wants a current newspaper from Sydney, Australia, the library will have to pay extra charges for the airmail edition or otherwise face an unacceptable delay in receiving current issues. Also, there is little point in paying for surface delivery of an Australian newspaper only to discover that the microfilm edition arrives sooner.

If a library wants to spread a meagre acquisitions budget amongst a large selection of newspapers, it will be much cheaper to subscribe to the paper copy than to the microfilm (for example, the Winnipeg *Free Press* in original format costs approximately $100.00 per year and the microfilm costs an estimated $700.00 annually). However, if the newspaper subscription is intended to help build a retrospective collection, then microfilm is the only practical format. The collecting of original newspapers which are intended to be kept indefinitely requires a serious commitment to preservation (temperature, humidity and light controls) and to conservation (de-acidification, lamination) and a careful consideration of library policy regarding user access to the collection. The reality of deterioration of original newspapers must be faced whenever they are lent to patrons, and many libraries routinely refuse access to originals except for very special reasons.

Although the advent of microfilm has greatly increased the availability of newspapers for research purposes, it has tended to obscure the very real differences between hard copy and film. If a scholar is studying newspapers as a physical format, for example, the history of paper-making or printing, microfilm will be of little use in such research. Content analysis of newspaper can also be rendered much more difficult if a researcher must work only from microfilm.

It is undeniable that reproductions from original newspapers are far superior to those made from microfilm, and this is particularly important if the material required is to be republished (in a book, or in an audiovisual format such as film or slides). Indeed, in the case of reproduction of photographs in newspapers, it is virtually impossible to get a clear picture from microfilm unless very sophisticated techniques are used.

These arguments are made under the assumption that the microfilm is of good quality and is complete. However, newspaper librarians quickly discover that far too much of the commercial microfilm that is produced is blurred or spotty, that issues have been filmed backwards, upside down, or have been left out altogether, and that issues used for filming have been rescued from a fire or used as insulation for the attic. This is not to mention the bibliographic nightmares which result from different companies filming parts of newspaper runs, overlapping dates with each other, mixing editions on the same reel, and even filming completely separate bibliographic entitities together. Acquisitions librarians learn soon which commercial micropublishers to trust and which ones to avoid buying from.

Unfortunately, however, micropublishers tend to have monopolies in their respective regions, and may in fact have contracts with the big newspaper chains (Thomson, Knight-Ridder are examples) to microfilm any or all of their newspapers. Librarians may have no choice but to order from these companies. It is advisable then to purchase such products only on approval. Commercial micropublishers should be encouraged to follow standards such as those written by the Library of Congress and the National Micrographics Association. Certainly the quality conscious companies are committed to them.

There are various selection tools for microforms, and many that are devoted specifically to newspapers in microform. Micropublishers such as Bell and Howell in Wooster, Ohio and Commonwealth Microfilm Library in Calgary, Alberta and Willowdale, Ontario, put out annual catalogs, and while their bibliographical accuracy is not always above reproach, they can generally be relied upon. The Library of Congress *Newspapers in Microform, 1948--1972* and its supplements, the *Register of Microform Masters*, and the British Library *Guide to Micropublications* are all examples of other sources to consult when considering the purchase of microfilm.

In general, the holder of the master negative as indicated in these sources is the company or institution which has the rights to sell positive (i.e., service) copies, but rights can change hands if a company goes out of business or if another company has the business acumen to win away the rights, so it is important to double-check before ordering. It has been known to happen that microfilm will be unidentifiable because the company or institution has failed to provide adequate target information on the film, or the film has been orphaned through the death of its parent company. This situation has caused much gnashing of teeth amongst selection and acquisitions librarians!

Before leaving the subject of the acquisitions of microforms, it is important to have some awareness of the types of microfilm available and the relative merits of each. Up until a few years ago, libraries and archives automatically purchased silver halide because of its proven archival quality and the assumption that the film was being bought for addition to a permanent collection. However, with the astronomical rise in silver prices in the past few years, libraries have had to reconsider their aversion to diazo and vesicular film because subscription renewal budgets cannot accommodate this blind allegiance to silver-based film. Aging tests done on diazo film have been positive, and as long as the master negative is preserved by the relevant company or institution, positive copies can always be made if deterioration of diazo film becomes a problem. The average library should not have to spend its meagre resources on expensive silver film.

Organizing the Collection

Newspapers are the best example of why serials librarians tend to retire early. There are frequent title changes, numerous mergers and absorptions, and many frequency changes. Moreover, there can be several different editions published within the same time frame, as well as many title variations involving the use of "popular" titles. For example, the *Washington Post* may be cited by readers simply as *The Post*, but what is the masthead title? And is there a variation in the running title and/or the title as given on the publisher's statement? And then there are titles which defy logic, with the favorite example being *Le Quotidien* ("The Daily") which of course was published weekly!

There are also changes in place of publication. This becomes very crucial for those newspapers which derive much of their value from their geographical area. There are even examples of newspaper which are published on trains or on board ships. This makes it impossible to pin down their place of publication.

Unfortunately, the cataloguing standards (AACR2, CONSER) do not deal adequately with the unique problems posed by the bibliographic jungle of newspapers. The index entry for newspapers in the *Anglo-American Cataloguing Rules* refers catalogers to the chapter on serials, and the emphasis is decidedly upon serial publications such as periodicals, magazines, newsletters and their ilk. The Library of Congress and the Organization of American Historians, under the sponsorship of the National Endowment for the Humanities, attempted, a few years ago, the production of their *Newspaper Cataloguing Manual*. This *Manual*, compiled by Elaine Woods for use by participating libraries in the U.S. Newspaper Project, was an attempt to apply the principles of AACR2, CONSER, ISBD--S and other standards to the cataloging of newspapers, but the final version has yet to be published.

Many libraries do not catalog their newspapers because they are often thought of as ephemeral material which will not be retained except on a current issue basis. Most newspapers, moreover, require original cataloging because there is little copy to be found in the cooperative serials databases and catalogs being produced now.

It is often easiest just to arrange original newspapers on the shelves alphabetically by title, and to shelve microfilm by sequential accession number with an accompanying finding aid by title. It is important, however, to provide adequate cross references to earlier and later titles, since exact newspaper titles are not often known by researchers. Also, access by place of publication is essential for the same reasons; users are just as apt to ask for a newspaper from Los Angeles as they are to ask for the *Times*.

Maintaining the Collection

The question of maintaining an original newspaper collection is usually a more urgent one than any consideration of the health and well-being of the microform collection. This is true because newsprint disintegrates much more quickly. Up until the mid- to late 19th century, newspapers were printed on paper with a high rag content. Examples of them still around today are in pristine condition. The Toronto *Globe* of July 1, 1867, Canada's Confederation, is in far better shape than its successor, the *Globe and Mail* for Canada's 50th birthday in 1917. Therefore, any serious attempt to preserve and conserve originals must concentrate on newspapers with a high acid content in their paper.

Proper temperature and humidity controls are essential, along with careful attention to lighting. Sunlight or any artificial light is deadly to newspapers, and so they should not be allowed to infiltrate newspaper shelving. It is also a good idea to lay newspaper flat, rather than folding them for placement into pamphlet boxes. Ideally they should be bound.

Users should be cautioned about the brittle newsprint which they are likely to encounter, and should be advised that special reprographic techniques may be necessary to minimize damage to the originals. Overhead photostat machines and photographs can solve the problem of requests for reproductions, although such services are likely to be more expensive than standard photocopying procedures. Although librarians are very much access- and service-oriented, they must be prepared to enforce strict rules on the use of originals, or their collections will not be preserved for use by future generations.

Conservation techniques such as de-acidification and lamination can be very effective with deteriorating newspapers, but they are extremely expensive and time-consuming. Moreover, there are few shops set up to handle conservation on what would inevitably be a large scale due to the frequency of publication of the average newspaper. Mass deacidification is just starting to come into its own, so it is still not practical for newspapers on a large scale.

Librarians will most often turn to microfilming as a preservation method. This technique should suit an average library's purposes. Microfilming involves the creation of a master negative from original newspapers, and as such, can be very expensive. The ideal solution is for a library to interest a commercial micropublisher in taking on the job. If the micropublisher can be assured of between three to five sales of positive copies, it is likely that the costs of filming will be underwritten by the company.

Microfilming is also best left to these companies (those which are reputable, of course) because they can take care of locating missing issues, devising good targets for the leader portion of each reel, arranging for copyright clearance and payment of royalties to the holders of the copyright, and finally, they can market the film and handle purchase orders.

Many successful cooperative microfilming projects have been undertaken, such as the ones by the Center for Research Libraries in Chicago, and the Ontario Colleges and Universities Libraries in Chicago, and the Ontario Colleges and Universities Libraries project to film Ontario ethnic newspapers. Such consortiums can be far more cost-effective for libraries than going it alone.

Accessing the Collection

Having alluded to and elaborated upon the many problems associated with the technical services side of a library's association with newspapers, it is now important to consider the rewards for perserverance, and there are many. Newspapers will yield an enormous wealth of information on any topic imaginable if reference skills are used in assisting patrons of the collection.

There is no problem at all if the user has the exact title and date of the required newspaper. It simply becomes a matter of verification to see that the newspaper is available in the collection (or elsewhere through interlibrary loan) and then to retrieve the newspaper. The mark of a good newspaper reference librarian is to be found in his/her ability to locate the needed article when told only that, for example, a Chinese cook was murdered somewhere in Western Canada in a lumber camp during the 1880s. It may then be necessary to check manuscript sources, or to seek out secondary sources, such as history of the pulp and paper industry in British Columbia, and perhaps even to consult accounts of Chinese immigration to Canada.

Obviously, the best reference source would be a newspaper index, but with the exception of indexes to the *New York Times* and *The Times* (London), there are very few retrospective indexes to the world's newspapers. Because the job is such a mammoth one, it is unlikely that anyone will ever undertake the task.

As a last resort, some researchers spend years in newspaper libraries, going through newspapers page by page, searching for the elusive piece of information which they feel sure is there somewhere. It is therefore encouraging to see the proliferation of newspaper indexes over the last few years. We can only hope that libraries will be able to support these fledgling efforts through paid subscriptions.

The developments in high technology in recent years have also made possible the application to computerized indexing of newspapers, and in some cases, to full-text retrieval, as for example, the InfoGlobe system developed by the Toronto *Globe and Mail*. This makes the traditional necessity of providing hard copy or microfilm back-up to citations almost obsolete, although it must be remembered that online printing of complete newspaper articles can be very expensive. There is no doubt, however, that computerized indexes have revolutionized the task of finding information in newspapers. They can save countless hours of staff time and user time in searching the actual newspapers.

For those libraries with major newspaper collections, such as the Library of Congress, the National Library of Canada, and the British Library, reference service for newspapers is provided. Although even these libraries cannot afford the time it takes for extensive searches if vague information is provided. Libraries will often maintain lists of professional researchers who are willing to search newspapers for a fee, and this can be especially helpful for scholars at a long distance, who cannot borrow the original newspapers, and who cannot afford a trip to the relevant library. These libraries also maintain records of unpublished newspaper indexes, of newspapers which have been microfilmed by local historical societies, or other similar information which could be useful to potential users.

Summary and Conclusions

Not every library will be able to afford to build and maintain newspaper collections. But it is important for reference librarians to be aware of the information resources which can be gleaned from newspapers. Although not thought of as such, newspapers can be just as precious to the senior citizen who must use his/her birth announcement in the local paper to qualify for social security benefits as incunabula can be to the rare books librarians or the antiquarian dealer. Even if the reference librarian is able to refer a user to another library's newspaper collection, or to procure a needed newspaper on interlibrary loan, the vital link in the information chain may be made.

A Note on Sources

Library literature is fairly sparse for anyone wishing to read further into newspaper librarianship and all its aspects. There are many studies on serials librarianship, and on microform use in the library, and on conservation, as well as on the history of particular newspapers, but very few articles or books bring together all of these threads.

My information for this article was gathered from my experience as a newspaper reference librarian, and later, as Head, Newspaper Section, National Library of Canada (inclusive dates for both positions, 1975--1980). Many impressions were also formed by a visit in 1979 to the Newspaper Section of the Library of Congress, and attendance at the Newspaper Cataloguing Workshop held at that time there.

Credit should be given to the Newspaper Division of the Special Libraries Association, which has striven to air the concerns of newspaper librarians and to find solutions for the many problems. Although this body has, in my opinion, tended to concentrate on the operations of libraries associated with actual newspapers, and with press clippings libraries, they are nevertheless performing a valuable cohesive function within the newspaper librarianship community.

COMPUTERIZED MANAGEMENT OF MICROFORMS

Nancy Patricia O'Brien

To provide adequate access to microforms, libraries must not only provide full cataloging, they must also provide indexing to individual collections. Utilizing computers to provide cataloging and indexing is possible with current technology. It is imperative that libraries act now in order to make the fullest use of their resources in microform. As budgets shrink, libraries can no longer justify purchasing or requesting on interlibrary loan materials which duplicate microform items in their collections but which are bibliographically inaccessible.

Historical Background

Since microforms were first made available to libraries, the control and accession of materials in microform has been an unresolved problem. Now that we have entered the computer age, that problem may be resolved by the utilization of computers in microform management. Monographs on microform has seldom caused problems related to bibliographic control. Like their paper counterparts, they are complete in themselves. However, in those cases where a set of items are related in subject matter, or when an ongoing serial is involved, the problems become manifold.

Full cataloging of microform sets in the past has been done by only a few libraries across the nation.[1] Despite an ARL study in the 1950s which recommended eye-legible internal bibliographic controls on microfilm, full standardized cataloging, and the creation of a bibliographic record of master negatives, little was done to follow through on those recommendations. It was several years before the *National Register of Microform Masters* was established. Even at that, however, the first volume was of questionable quality.[2]

A later ARL study by Felix Reichmann and Josephine Tharpe reiterated the recommendations made in the earlier study. Tharpe and Reichmann concluded that the "use of an entirely new and revolutionary production method such as microphotography demands an innovative bibliographic tool if the selection and processing of microforms are to be adequately controlled. Such a tool [would combine] computer and microfilm."[3] Tharpe and Reichmann recommended the creation of a machine-readable index to access microform series in individual libraries. Such an index could produce printouts in microfilm, tape or book form.[4] Their final conclusion was that a national machine-readable index of microforms, capable of providing a complete index for microform collections in specific libraries, should be developed.[5] Appendix two of the Reichmann and Tharpe volume is a methodology for utilizing computers to produce an index to materials contained in microform sets. The suggested formats for those indexes are hard-copy or microfilm.[6] Ironically, the idea of an on-line index was not considered.

Even in ARL's most recent acknowledgment of the need for standardized cataloging of microforms through the facilities of bibliographic utilities, the idea of creating a computer-controlled retrieval (CCR) system has not been discussed widely. Although the ARL study group on the "Bibliographic Control of Microforms" did "entertain . . . that avenue of inquiry," it was decided that cooperative cataloging of microforms utilizing the national bibliographic utilities was the primary concern of the study.[7]

It is unfortunate that a closer examination by libraries of the possibilities of a computer/microfilm system has not been undertaken. As early as 1970, the business world was forecasting the interface between microforms and computers. Hardware systems were developed which could use a microform memory as well as the traditional magnetic memory. This meant that 20 million pages of information (or 900 billion bits) on microfilm could be accessed in seconds from a number of remote terminals. Microfilm memories could store 20 times more information than the magnetic tape at a similar cost.[8] The business world was quick to appreciate the advantages of such a system. Libraries have yet to deal with the implications for information sciences.

To the librarian and the library patron, the benefits of such a system are phenomenal. The day when a library patron can approach a computer terminal (CRT), request a document and have the screen display the actual document is nearing rapidly. A highly developed microfiche system is available now which provides that kind of service. In fact, the system, Automated Records Management System (ARMS), is so sophisticated that an ARMS CRT terminal can be "interfaced to a word processing unit, an electronic mail system or a distributed processing network (or all three)."[9]

Most libraries do not need such a complex set of functions,

unless used in personnel and administrative areas. A "simple" system to provide on-line selection, location and display of information contained on microform will adequately serve the current needs of library users. And, besides, such a system would be available to libraries only at great cost. As a consequence, the likelihood of automated retrieval systems for microforms appearing in libraries, especially in times of shrinking budgets, is almost nonexistent. Until the expense of creating adequate indexes to microforms is less than the cost of locating materials elsewhere, libraries will continue to use traditional methods for accessing microforms.

The plan developed by ARL to cooperatively catalog microforms using bibliographic utilities is in response to the need for more information at less cost to the individual library. It has taken years for a national plan to be implemented, although recommendations for full cataloging were presented soon after microforms appeared in libraries.[10] As Simon and Gerber point out, the time required for U.S. industry, commerce and the professions to fully accept a new mechanical process is twenty years.[11] Hence, we can probably expect twenty years from the development of a computerized retrieval system for microforms, libraries will adopt such an on-line system.

Microform/Computer Systems

As mentioned earlier, microform/computer retrieval systems already exist. However, because of format, it is much easier to interface a computer system with microfiche, rather than microfilm. Because microfiche are laid out in a standardized grid pattern, the computer can easily pinpoint a particular page or paragraph.

Microfilm is not so easily accessible. In order to retrieve material on a reel of microfilm, it is necessary to code items. The individual documents are coded in such a way that a computer can scan, locate and display an item automatically. Various coding systems are available which use bars (similar to the Universal Product Code) or blips (a photographic mark under each frame), as well as more simplistic devices such as eye-legible marks. The key is to tag individual frames so that a computer can identify and retrieve a particular document or page using those marks.

Manual or semi-automatic systems which use blips or eye-legible marks generally rely on a machine or on manual counting of marks from one document to the next. That type of system necessitates a good memory or a machine which can adapt easily to moving forwards and backwards, subtracting or adding frames as required to reach the needed document. Most importantly, such a system, as well as a fully automated system requires an excellent index.

When dealing with microform serials or sets, the problem has always been in accessing the information contained in microform. Early microform sets were generally developed around a bibliography of printed books, and consequently, an index, of sorts, already existed.[12] Micropublishers sometimes provided printed guides. But there has been little consistency in the kinds or quality of indexes provided. The preparation of an adequate index for a microform set or serial is costly and time-consuming. With these considerations in mind, the use of a computer to create an index becomes more attractive and viable. The realization that a computer-produced index can be made available on magnetic tape, microform or in book form is an added inducement.

To create an index, it is necessary to tag individual sections (generally frames) for identification by the computer. Creating a data file with tagged microfilm which has been placed on a cassette requires inserting the cassette into a terminal, placing the terminal in an on-line mode, and keying in a predetermined accession code. Once the documents are indexes, the data will be sorted and merged into a master file. An alternative form of entering data is to use keypunching and interface with a COM tape.[13]

The methods of creating an on-line index sound simple in terms of creating the data and providing it to the user. Whether such a system will satisfy a cataloger is another question. An on-line index to microforms would identify available documents; however, it would not provide a complete history of the original printed item including pagination and size. If micropublishers provided indexes on magnetic tape, it might make access easier for the patron. But unless the availability of the microform copy is advertised in the catalog (paper or on-line), the patron will remain unaware of the existence of a particular item in the library collection.

Current Developments

The management of serials or sets in microform is being addressed again at the national level at long last. The Association of Research Libraries is currently involved in a study on the bibliographic control of microforms which will result in the publication of the study, its conclusions, and recommendations. A national program for cooperative cataloging of microform sets is already in the implementation stage because of this study.[14]

In addition, the ALA Subcommittee to Monitor the Quality of Micropublications has developed a draft of "Guidelines for an Acceptable Microform Publication." The Subcommittee, an ad hoc body under the ALA Resources and Technical Services Division's Micropublishing Committee, is in the final stages of developing the guidelines for use by both librarians and micropublishers. The intent of the publication is to provide guides to the technical quality of micropublications which are acceptable to librarians. Quality of content is not considered in the document.[15] By providing guidelines for acceptable means of bibliographic control, it is hoped that standard procedures and practices will be implemented by commercial and institutional micropublishers.

Both ARL and the Subcommittee address the question of bibliographic control of microforms. Both groups offer solutions to different aspects of the problem. ARL is concerned with the vast quantity of uncataloged or partially cataloged microforms that exist in libraries nationwide. The Subcommittee to Monitor the Quality of Micropublications is concerned that microforms meet certain criteria before they reach the consumer. Some of those criteria deal with bibliographic control (e.g., microfilm targets, guides to collections), while others deal with advertising, packaging and related marketing questions.

Although the Subcommittee "Guidelines" broach the topic of indexing more than does the ARL study, both groups leave this question for later consideration. In discussing bibliographic control of microforms, there are two critical areas. One is access within the library system and the other is access within the individual microform set or serial. In both areas of bibliographic control, the computer will play a major role. In some instances, full cataloging of a microform set will obviate the need for an index. An index can oftentimes provide information not easily obtainable in a catalog, however, and is a desirable asset to a microform collection of materials linked together by subject. The technology to provide adequate indexes to microform collections is currently available utilizing a microform/computer interface. The necessity of providing both full cataloging and adequate indexes to microform collections requires further consideration.

Resolution

The solution to the problem lies in both cooperative cataloging of microform sets (retrospective and current) as proposed by ARL and the use of an on-line index and retrieval system for individual microform sets. Using a combination of these systems, a patron might first locate a needed item in a monographic set of microforms using an on-line catalog, or, if necessary, some type of paper catalog. After ascertaining that the item is available and identifying its classification code, the patron could request the item through a computer-controlled retrieval system and have it displayed on a CRT. Ideally, this process would occur at one CRT terminal; practically, it would probably require two steps and two systems.

A sophisticated user initially might try the microform system, eliminating the first step. However, such a user would have to have a sound knowledge of the library's holdings in microform materials. Also, in that instance, microform would be, presumably, the preferred format. If the catalog was accessed first, it might locate the requested item in one of several formats including paper. In many instances, the paper copy may be desired for research purposes, or for portability. Consequently, for computer access, microforms first should be fully cataloged for integration into a library's record of holdings. Then they should be indexed for use in an on-line retrieval system. In those instances when a microform serial or set is indexed first, it can assist the cataloger a great deal in providing adequate detailed information about the location of a particular document and the content. Providing access to the index is crucial. The index is useful only if it too can be located or is part of the microform system. The consensus in the library community towards microforms is summarized by C. Edward Carroll in the following statement, "cataloged materials are used; non-cataloged materials are not."[16] The same cannot be said about indexed materials. Use of microform materials which lack indexing is extremely difficult but does not deter the persistent patron.

In the ARL study on bibliographic control of microforms, it was determined that the creation of a national index to microform collections would be detrimental to the recommendation for cooperative cataloging. It was feared that many libraries might choose to utilize such an index rather than fully catalog microform sets.[17] The attractive possibility of selecting a relatively inexpensive method of partially resolving the problem of bibliographic control could undermine efforts to resolve the more pressing need for full cataloging. Individual computer packages which provide indexing to microform collections *would* be compatible to full cataloging of microforms, particularly if a retrieval capability was incorporated into the computer system. A national index would be competitive not complementary to the full cataloging of microforms.

Cataloging an ongoing microform program such as *American Fiction* without providing analytics is not truly cataloging the set. While the ARL study, "Bibliographic Control of Microforms," undertaken by ISCI (Information Systems Consultants, Inc.), addresses the major problem of providing analytics for numerous microform programs, it still does not provide the type of subject access that is needed in an individual microform set. Even providing analytics does not solve the varied difficulties of locating works or passages that can be attributed to a particular author or which fall to a certain subject area. It will be necessary still to provide an index to microform serials or sets which can quickly pinpoint such information.

Such an index should be on-line because of the rapid retrieval; the amount of additional information which a computer can store; and because it consolidates information in an attractive format. In addition, with a fully automated retrieval system, the patron never needs to physically handle the microform. This can be an incentive both to the frustrated user trying to rewind a reel of microfilm which has been left on backwards by the preceding user and also to the librarian tired of repairing smudged, broken microfilm. Although there will be certain small collections of microfiche or film which are easier to handle manually, the majority of microforms can be indexed in one system which also has a retrieval and display capability. In fact, the advantage to the user trying to locate a particular work and finding variant editions in different microform sets is obvious. Not only will the library's holdings be enhanced if it offers complete information about microform holdings, but its reputation will also be boosted.

Conclusion

Much has been said in the past few decades about the importance of providing bibliographic control of microforms. ARL's project on cooperative cataloging of microforms, if funded, will provide many solutions to the problem. The project looks sufficiently to the future so that long-term, rather than interim, solutions are being provided. The project's scope is limited, however, and consequently, there are several problems remaining, chief among these being the provision of adequate indexes.

In a National Micrographics Association (NMA) publication which discussed microform indexing systems it is noted that the trend is to use computers to produce and manipulate indexes, although there are still some effective manual indexing systems.[18] Unfortunately, the computer all too often is used to produce the index in book or microfilm format. The ultimate irony appears in Robert Bland's 1979 article, "Quiet Crisis," which forecasts a paper card catalog of microfilm holdings and a machine-readable catalog for print items.[19] His prediction is based on the lack of machine-readable records for microform collections, and on his despair that the information world would ever listen to his plea to develop an organized program to cooperatively catalog microforms and create machine-readable records.[20]

In October, 1980, ARL presented a report which made many of the same recommendations as had Robert Bland. Although ARL appears to have acted quickly, in truth the "quiet crisis" had been going on for some time, and the technology and professional cooperation are now finally at a point where the problem can be addressed with some hope of resolution. There is little doubt that the ARL project will be accomplished. A few ruffled feathers over the cataloging (AACR2 or an interim method) may be the only casualties encountered. Unfortunately, the project will take time, and as the project starts, quantum leaps in computer technology are being made.

The ARL project may be outdated before it is completed, and new methods of accessing microforms will be in use by a business world which demands speedy, but cost effective retrieval of information. Systems such as ARMS already outdistance the most advanced of library technologies handling microforms. Because of monetary considerations, few libraries will be able to implement systems which interface the computer and microforms at any time in the near future.

Librarians should be aware of what the future holds and systems which are already available. ARMS has already been mentioned as one of the most advanced microfiche CCR systems. The computer-controlled retrieval process provides individual pages from a microform set through computer intervention either in response to a user request or because of a computer-monitored situation. The microform is retrieved from the file by the computer and displayed on a screen which is either a microform reader or an electronic representation of the microfilmed image.[21] In the case of ARMS, the system selects a microfiche at the user's request, presents it to a special camera which digitizes the microimage and sends the information to a computer disc. Once on disc, the image is sent and displayed at a high-resolution terminal.[22] An earlier system developed by Ragen retrieved roll film automatically and was equipped with a minicomputer disc storage, film storage and film-entry devices.[23] In 1975, a system which combined CRT-generated images with micro-projected images on the same plasma screen was reported. The less sophisticated systems which transmit microimages to CRT monitors were also available at that time.[24]

Computer Input from Microfilm (CIM) which is the conversion of images contained on film to a machine-readable form, has been discussed in the literature, but not nearly so widely as COM.[25] Many of the applications of CIM, particularly in the library world, have not yet been addressed. In terms of indexing a microform set, a computer program which can access magnetic tape rather than microform has phenomenal advantages. The conversion from film to tape also will, unfortunately, have phenomenal costs attached.

In an excellent summary work published by NMA, F.I. Bolnick points out that while self-contained computer/microfilm retrieval systems exist and are being improved rapidly, the basic premise of having two separate systems which interface when needed can be advantageous. Advantages include the option of using standard economical equipment for each system; the ability of the computer and microfilm systems to perform independently of one another; the capability of one computer system controlling multiple retrieval units; and the utilization of computer programs to provide additional links to microform retrieval.[26]

Libraries also will find it advantageous to have two separate systems. One system can be the on-line catalog, the other a computer controlled retrieval system. Using a CRT, both systems might be accessed from the same termianl. The software will be accessed separately.

Forecasts

Some of the forecasts which have been made previously regarding microforms include Veaner's belief that "computers and microforms will have merged into a continuum of information processing tools which shall give us the best of both."[27] A more recent prediction by W. Carl Jackson forecasts that improved bibliographic access will increase the use of microforms and create a major demand for auxiliary services connected by microforms.[28]

Both predictions have already been proven true. Computer/microform systems do exist which can provide excellent control of data. And such systems are constantly being improved. In those institutions where microforms are adequately cataloged, there is an increased use of microforms.[29]

An additional prediction being offered in this paper is that in less than twenty years, libraries will have cooperatively cataloged the major microform sets and will be using computer-controlled retrieval and display systems — those same systems which are being used currently by industry and business. Libraries have advanced sufficiently so that the twenty years once required for the professions to accept a new mechanical process has been shortened considerably. Acceptance of new procedures is occurring much more rapidly than ever before, and technological innovations and the accompanying advantages have created their own demand in the information sciences.

In using computer/microform systems, libraries will be able to provide the optimum amount of information available on microform to their clientele. Despite the fact that computer technologies are capable of providing adequate access now, few libraries can boast that they are able to retrieve all materials on microform using the card catalog. A marriage of full cataloging and computer/microform systems will provide the major solution to the bibliographic control of microforms.

NOTES

1. "Bibliographic Control of Microforms: A Planning Study for the Association of Research Libraries. Final Report," n.p., 1980, p. 6. (Typewritten.)

2. Ibid., pp. 8–9.

3. Felix Reichmann and Josephine Tharpe, *Bibliographic Control of Microforms* (Westport, CT: Greenwood Press, 1972), p. 5.

4. Ibid., p. 12.

5. Ibid., pp. 31–32.

6. Henriette D. Avram and Harry Gochman, "A Machine-Readable Index for Microsets," in Reichmann and Tharpe, *Bibliographic Control of Microforms*, pp. 46–47.

7. Telephone interview with Richard Boss, Information Systems Consultants, Inc., Bethesda, MD, 10 June 1981.

8. "Computer/Microfilm Systems," *Automation* 17 (March 1970): 10.

9. David Fain and Garrett Gruener, "The Automated Records Management System," *Journal of Micrographics* 12 (May/June 1979): 305.

10. "Bibliographic Control of Microforms: A Planning Study," p. 6.

11. Charles K. Simon and Donald L. Gerber, "Fully Automated Records Management," *Journal of Micrographics* 12 (September/October 1978): 54.

12. "Bibliographic Control of Microforms: A Planning Study," p. 6.

13. John M. Griffin, "On-line Microfilm," in *Proceedings of the Twenty-First Annual Meeting and Convention*, ed. by Deborah D. Daley (Silver Spring, MD: National Microfilm Association, 1972), pp. 72–73.

14. "News from the Field–ARL Plan on Microforms," *RTSD Newsletter* 6 (May/June 1981): 32.

15. [American Library Association, Resources Section, Resources and Technical Services Division, Micropublishing Committee, Subcommittee to Monitor the Quality of Micropublications], "Guidelines for an Acceptable Microform Publication, Draft 3," n.p., n.d., p. 1. (Typewritten.)

16. C. Edward Carroll, "Bibliographic Control of Microforms: Where Do We Go from Here?" *Microform Review* 7 (November 1978): 322.

17. "Bibliographic Control of Microforms: A Planning Study," p. 40.

18. Marilyn Courtot, *Microform Indexing and Retrieval Systems* (Silver Spring, MD: National Microfilm Association, n.d.), p. 20.

19. Robert Bland, "Quiet Crisis: Bibliographic Control and Machine-Readable Records for Microforms," *North Carolina Libraries* 37 (Winter 1979): 14.

20. Ibid., p. 16.

21. Arthur A. Teplitz, "Computer-Controlled Retrieval: A Primer," *Journal of Micrographics* 5 (September 1971): 36–37.

22. Fain and Gruener, "Automated Records Management System," p. 305.

23. Franklin I. Bolnick, *Micrographic Retrieval – Computer Interface*, NMA Special Interest Package 1 (Silver Spring, MD: National Micrographics Association, 1976), p. 7.

24. Frank Malabarba, "Microfilm Information Systems (MIS): A Data Base Alternative," *Journal of Micrographics* 9 (September/October 1975): 7.

25. Roger Holland, "CIM – The Present and the Future," *Microdoc* 15 (1976): 52.

26. Bolnick, "Micrographic Retrieval – Computer Interface," p. 8.

27. "Looking Ahead, Forecasts, Old and New," in *Studies in Micropublishing, 1853–1976: Documentary Sources*, ed. by Allen B. Veaner, Microform Review Series in Library Micrographics Management, vol. 2 (Westport, CT: Microform Review, 1977), p. 441.

28. W. Carl Jackson, "Bibliographic Access to Microforms: On the Threshhold?" *Microform Review* 9 (Winter 1980): 31.

29. Carroll, "Bibliographic Control of Microforms," p. 322.

GOVERNMENT PUBLICATIONS AS SERIALS

Steven D. Zink

Thousands of governmental agencies around the world issue tens of thousands of serial publications each year. In fact, the best estimate indicates that approximately 70 to 80 percent of all government publishing appears in the form of serials.[1]

The variety of material produced is as staggering as the number. Perhaps the largest category is represented by technical reports. Single agencies such as the United States National Aeronautics and Space Administration or the Department of Energy produce dozens of technical reports series. Nearly as prevalent are the numerous annual reports of both agencies and subagencies. Monographic series are also common in almost every level of government publishing.

The most impressive component of government serial publishing, however, is the extraordinary number of periodicals produced by governmental entities. For example, the U.S. Department of Defense, in 1972, admitted to producing 1,402 periodicals, excluding newspapers.[2]

The most obvious uses of government periodicals are either for in-house information dissemination or for public relations. To be sure, these are very important roles; however, the titles are not so narrowly limited. Many government periodicals are prominent in various professional and scholarly disciplines. The *Monthly Labor Review*, for example, has long been the most prominent journal in its field. Many governmental periodicals have independent editorial boards and are virtually indistinguishable from publications of the private sector. Their widespread acceptance is graphically shown by the inclusion of ten in the current *Reader's Guide to Periodical Literature*, the most popular index to general interest periodicals.

It is not difficult to understand why governments in the publishing business are attracted to serials as the preferred format. The central purpose of most publications is quick dissemination of information. Hence, most of the total funds expended on a given publication are in the compiling, writing, editing, and actual production processes, and little attention has traditionally been paid to bibliographic control. By numerically designating publications as they appear, an agency provides a rudimentary means of identifying its materials at a nominal cost. As a result, many series titles are artificially contrived, provide no indication of the subject matter of the titles therein, and are " . . . simply held together by symbols which enable them to take on the character of serial publications."[3]

As should be evident from the preceding paragraphs, the number and possible complexities of government serials are immense. The balance of this chapter will seek only to survey the technical and public service aspects of government serials, and cannot be a comprehensive treatment of the subject. (For further information one should consult the various sources noted.) The reader will observe that greater emphasis will be placed upon periodicals than on serials, in general, and that publications of the U.S. government will be the most prominently discussed.

One other caveat is also offered. For the purposes of discussion it is assumed that government publications are housed separately from the general library collection, and that unique concerns confront individuals faced with this situation. The familiar argument of whether government publications should be housed separately or integrated into the main library collection will not be entertained at length in the traditional manner. The very important relationships between a library's general collection and its government publications will be discussed in terms of integration of bibliographic information, not in terms of physical integration. The currently-available specialized tools, as well as the expertise necessary to assure maximum utilization of government publications, make physical integration a disservice in any institution with a substantial number of government publications.

Bibliographic Control

As much as government-produced serials may be similar to serials produced in the private sector, there are a number of areas in which differences are clearly evident. Perhaps one of the most obvious divergences is in the area of bibliographic control. Government publications as an entity have traditionally received poor treatment in standard bibliographic tools. In recent years improvements have been made at all levels. The evolution of the treatment of government serials is evident in the increasingly better coverage of *New Serial Titles* over that of the basic *Union List of Serials*.[4] *Ulrich's International Periodical Directory* also represents an impressive listing of serials, specifically periodicals. A particularly valuable aspect of the *Ulrich's Directory* is an appendix of periodicals issued by international agencies.

Perhaps the most comprehensive listing of serials produced by the United States government (even though sadly lacking in criteria for inclusion) is to be found in the "Serials Supplement" to the *Monthly Catalog of United States Government Publications*. Bibliographic control of state-issued government publications, on the other hand, is fragmented. The traditional single source for all state publications (serial and non-serial) is the Library of Congress' *Monthly Checklist of State Publications* which provides a simple listing of titles by state.[5] More recently, Information Handling Services has undertaken a comprehensive effort for bibliographic control in its *State Publications Index*. Greenwood Press produces a commercial tool, *Index to Current Urban Documents*, which attempts to maintain bibliographic control over elusive serial, as well as non-serial, municipal documents.

Automation promises to greatly improve bibliographic control. One example of such promise is a current project being conducted at the University of California-Berkeley, the University of California-Los Angeles, and Stanford University. In 1978, these three schools received a grant under Title II--C of the Higher Education Act to create a machine-readable serials database. In the course of the project over 40,000 government document serial titles are expected to be converted using as a primary authority the national standards promulgated in the CONSER edition of the Library of Congress' *MARC Serials Editing Guide*.[6] Thus some uniformity in government serials so useful in cooperative collection development and interlibrary lending will soon be available.

Selection

Perhaps one of the greatest advances in government publications librarianship has been the proliferation of serial review sources. Even though most large collections of government publications are acquired on a depository basis and reviews may not be needed for selection purposes, they still serve a critical role. First of all, traditional library reviewing tools have not adequately covered government serials for those non-depository institutions seeking information before purchase of a title. More important, any review provides a useful function as an adjudicator of quality and as an informational outlet for utilization of the title.

Although for any one title traditional review sources should be checked, one's best bet when dealing with government publications is to check the various columns and journals dealing with the subject. As the two major government documents journals, *Documents to the People (DttP)*, and *Government Publications Review* frequently offer news and reviews of serials; *Government Publications Review* in its accompanying "Acquisitions Guide" is particularly well suited for reviews.

Regular columns or articles which occasionally review government serials appear in the *Wilson Library Bulletin, Microform Review, Serials Librarian, RQ*, and *Booklist*. The "Government Publications" column in *Reference Services Review (RSR)* is a source of reviews for non-periodical government serial titles while the "Government Publications" column in *Serials Review* is specifically devoted to a thematic analysis of periodicals produced by government entities.[7]

Acquisition

The two most prevalent methods of acquiring government publications are through a depository program or through traditional vendors. Clearly, most serial titles produced by government agencies are included in the various depository programs already in operation by state, federal, and international agencies. The size and diversity of these programs is overwhelming. For example, the current depository program administered by the United States Government Printing Office numbers nearly 1,400 libraries and distributes over 50,000 different titles each year.[8] Of course, popular serials are available through most familiar library vendors.

In addition to the two previously noted methods of acquisition, the variety of methods for acquiring government serials titles is almost limitless. Until just recently many government serials could be acquired free upon request. Regrettably, the fiscal austerity of the past few years has played havoc with this method of acquisition. However even though the gold mine may not be as lucrative as it was in the past, it should not be ignored. There are still some complimentary titles to be had.[9]

As the number of active mailing lists has dwindled, the sales pro grams at all levels of government have geared up to meet and to encourage the demand. Most government entities have subscription services and are willing to set up standing orders for customer convenience. For example, the U.S.G.P.O. recently began accepting major bank credit cards for purchases in its bookstores throughout the country and for sales by mail.

Once the sale of government serials and documents in general became commonplace, a number of private entrepreneurs entered the field providing not only copies of titles for a price, but also insuring completeness and excellent access tools. The undisputed leader in reproducing government publications for sale is the Congressional Information Service, Inc. (CIS).

Although CIS does not deal exclusively with government serials,

by the very nature of the prominence of serials within government publications as a whole, CIS makes available hundreds of *serial* titles. The Congressional Information Service, Inc. currently offers for purchase in microfiche all Congressional materials (serial and otherwise) from the most current to the very earliest.[10] Another CIS set (*American Statistics Index (ASI)*) offers a massive microfiche collection of federal statistical publications which includes serials virtually unobtainable otherwise.

Statistical state and university research publications are available through the Congressional Information Service (*Statistical Reference Index (SRI)*). (Specific mention is made of these sets in a following section.) CIS offers these materials on a variety of bases, including the purchase of individual issues or titles on demand. Various companies have emulated CIS's remarkable efforts. Taken as a whole, these massive microfiche sets account for a substantial percentage of many government publications departments' acquisitions budgets and have become a principal means for departments to acquire serial titles.[11]

Maintenance of the Collection

A major government publications collection today can easily acquire 100,000 items annually. Obviously, recording and suitably maintaining such an influx of materials is no small task. The type of record keeping required depends upon the make-up of the collection and the mission and nature of the institution.[12] The lack of uniformity within governmental series frequently poses problems. For the most part, periodicals can easily be accounted for on standard check-in cards.

Other serials, however, may be more difficult to record. Many institutions will simply check them off on cards; others may find it necessary or useful to record additional information or may want them cataloged and analyzed. All of these procedures are costly and time-consuming. Advances in serial control through the use of automation have been seen in recent years, and it is only a matter of time before these methods will be widely fitted to better suit and more economically serve recordkeeping requirements in government publications departments.

One problem with serials, in general, is particularly worrisome in regards to government serials. Invariably issues or volume numbers will be missing and require claiming or outright replacement. Most depository systems at all levels of government have a mechanism for claiming missing publications. Unfortunately, due to limited printing runs, it is occasionally quite difficult to locate an extant copy of a specific title. When such a case arises it is frequently wise to attempt to contact an agency directly.

An alternative is to nurture a close relationship with a good bookdealer who specializes in dealing with government publications.[13] The cooperative Universal Serials and Book Exchange also deals in government publications and may be of some help. For replacement of U.S. documents, the Documents Expediting Project of the Library of Congress provides an excellent service to member institutions in locating missing serial or periodical titles.[14]

Another important facet of documents collection maintenance is binding or microform substitution of non-current volumes. Almost every depository system stipulates that the publications deposited be well-maintained.[15] Yet surprisingly little has been written about the procedures or philosophy of binding government publications.[16] Traditionally, government publications departments have received woefully inadequate binding budgets and hence have bound minimally, while at the same time the prevailing library philosophy may have been that no title could be entered into the general library collection unbound. Such limited funds make it even more imperative for a government publications department to have a binding policy in order that priorities will be met and that binding will be uniform throughout the collection and over a period of time.

Due to space considerations and vast growth, many government publications departments have forged ahead into the arena of microform substitution[17] Money often appears more easily won for this space-saving technique of retention than for binding purposes. Obviously, serials and periodicals are the most likely candidates for which to substitute microform. Most prominent government periodicals and many large series are available in microform either on an individual basis or as a set. For example, all titles included in the *Index to U.S. Government Periodicals* are available in a microfiche set. All titles in the *American Statistics Index* and in the *CIS Index* are also available in microfiche.[18] The U.S. Serial Set, *Federal Register*, and *Official Gazette of the U.S. Patent and Trademark Office* (to name only a few) are available in a variety of formats — microfiche, microfilm, Readex microprint. State, local, international, and even non-governmental organizational materials are also available in a variety of microform products.[19]

Most government publications departments do not have to worry about future conversion to microfiche — this decision is being made by the issuing or distributing agencies. The United States Government Printing Office is leading the way in providing microfiche rather than paper copy. The original motivation to use microfiche was a desire to realize a budget savings as well as to assuage documents librarians' cries for critically-needed space savings. The future holds the promise of even more microform in an effort to offset the effects of federal budget slashing. The challenges this will pose to the documents librarian are enormous as the traditional documents collection is necessarily transformed, at least in part, to a microform reading area.

Utilizing the Collection

As is true with every informational product, government serials, once collected and shelved, are of little value unless they are put into the hand of individuals who will be able to utilize their contents. If the governmentally-produced serials are not housed separately and are treated indistinguishably from other materials of like format, the problem of access should be no different than in the case of the non-governmental materials. If, however, they are housed separately, it is incumbent upon the staff of the collection to see that the materials do not suffer from lack of use especially as the result of patron ignorance about such collections.

This widespread lack of awareness of government publications is what has earned them the dubious distinction of being dubbed " . . . the most neglected and under utilized information resource available to the public."[20] Various efforts must be undertaken to combat such departmental obscurity. Whatever the setting, prominent exhibits, displays, handouts, and publicity in general are useful to catch the attention of potential users. An attractive and comfortable browsing area in which patrons may leisurely view current popular periodical titles is a necessary corrective to the frequent perception that government material is simply archival in nature. The variety of possible approaches to informing the public of the value of government publications is virtually limitless. Fortunately, the professional literature has a growing body of material on the subject.[21]

Promotion is important; suitable and efficient access is essential. A long-standing argument of many librarians has been that government serials, particularly periodicals, should not be housed separately for they are overlooked and underutilized in a separate collection. This agument has died hard despite the fact that separate collections of all government publications offer expertise essential to the material's full potential use; related lesser-known material is at hand; and indexes and abstracts are of far higher quality and complexity than those which are usually found in a general reference area. Nevertheless, it is a fact that certain well-known titles may tend to be overlooked in special, separate collections. This need not be. Certainly all government periodicals which are indexed by commercial indexing services should have their holdings and location in a library's public service list. At least two efforts to prepare such a basic list of

U.S. government periodicals so indexed are readily available.[22]

In addition, all major series should be entered into the library's public catalog. If the series is monographic in nature, analytics should be prepared. The document classification number (Superintendent of Documents, UN, Swank, or other schemes) can easily be entered in the classification location on the card. The physical location of the material may be designated above or below the call number.[23]

Even if indexed periodicals and major series are so identified, the use of government series in research and development is so great and current indexing and abstracting services are so comprehensive that lesser-known series are now frequently cited in certain tools in the reference area. The *Public Affairs Information Service (P.A.I.S.)*, the *Environment Index*, the *Energy Index*, and the various "Citation Indexes"[24] are excellent examples of titles which frequently produce citations to government serials that cannot be effectively recorded in a public catalog or serials list.[25]

In all such instances every effort should be made to alert the index user to the availability of these materials in a government publications collection. Perhaps the most efficient way is to place a series of laminated signs on the index tables where these tools are located. The most unfortunate aspect of failing to do any of the above integration of bibliographic records is that it does not penalize the totally uninitiated patron who will normally seek help anyway and be directed to the government publications department. Instead, it will hinder the patron who has gained enough savvy and independence to proceed from an index to the public catalog or a serials list. If a title is not therein indicated, the patron may assume that the library does not own the publication.

Even though general reference tools have made some recent advances in including government materials, indexing is still inadequate. Fewer than forty percent of all of the titles recorded in the "Serials Supplement" of the *Monthly Catalog of United States Government Publications* are indexed anywhere.[26] Yet, specialized tools for dealing with government publications have made extraordinary strides. Progress in the area of U.S. government periodicals has been the most impressive. Beginning in the early 1970s, two indexes began commercial production and changed the nature of access to government periodicals. The first of these is the *Index to U.S. Government Periodicals (IUSGP)*.

Produced by Infordata International, Inc. of Chicago, *IUSGP* indexes, in a manner and format roughly analogous to the *Readers' Guide to Periodical Literature*, approximately 175 government periodicals, many of which are not indexed elsewhere. The popularity and use of this index in government publications collections have grown enormously to the point at which at least one use study found it to be the single most utilized documents access tool.[27]

Another tool which has helped revolutionize government periodical access is the previously discussed *American Statistics Index (ASI)*. Produced by the Congressional Information Service, Inc., the *ASI* indexes and extensively abstracts, among other things, periodicals which contain significant statistical information. One might expect that the *Index to U.S. Government Periodicals* and the *American Statistics Index* would significantly overlap in coverage. On the contrary, they complement each other quite well.[28]

The Congressional Information Service, Inc., has also introduced the *Statistical Reference Index (SRI)*. Similar to *ASI*, *SRI* indexes and abstracts non-federal government statistical material, including state and university serial publications. CIS is currently developing a similar sophisticated access tool for international statistical publications.

A government publications department may be the closest a library comes to having a special library within a library. The multitude of duties (processing, circulation, classification, promotion, instruction, binding, reference) and variety of materials (monographs, serials, periodicals, microforms) bear this out. Yet, as distinctive as a government publications department is, it is obvious that a great deal of commonality exists between the management of serials and the management of government publications. Certainly, one would expect that a closer relationship between the two departments would not only be possible but highly beneficial to serials and government publications librarians, alike.

NOTES

1. Thomas D. Gillies, "Document Serials, Technical Reports, and the National Bibliography," ed. Walter C. Allen (Urbana: University of Illinois, Graduate School of Library Science, 1969), 146; The term serials in this chapter is used in the broadest possible sense. For further discussion of the definition of a serial see: Doris M. Carson, "What Is a Serial Publication?" *The Journal of Academic Librarianship* 3 (September 1977): 206–209; Andrew D. Osborn, *Serial Publications: Their Place and Treatment in Libraries*, 2d ed., rev. (Chicago: American Library Association, 1973), 3–19.

2. Joe Morehead, "The Pentagon's Magazine Publishing Empire," *The Serials Librarian* 5 (Fall 1980): 7.

3. Osborn, *Serial Publications*, 388.

4. Gillies, "Document Serials," 146.

5. David Parish, review of *Monthly Checklist of State Publications* in a forthcoming issue of *Reference Services Review*.

6. Barbara Houghton (Serials Division, Stanford University), letter to Steven D. Zink, 26 March 1981.

7. Major U.S. serials are described and evaluated in: Nancy Patton Van Zant, *Selected U.S. Government Series: A Guide for Public and Academic Libraries* (Chicago: American Library Association, 1978).

8. "News from GPO," *Documents to the People (DttP)* 9 (May 1981): 86.

9. For example see: Myoung J. Chung, "Embassy Newsletters as Information Sources of Current Affairs," *Government Publications Review* 7A: 329–332; Steven D. Zink, *U.S. Government Publications Catalogs* (New York: Special Libraries Association, 1981); The Documents Expediting Project of the Library of Congress, upon request, attempts to place member institutions on agency mailing lists.

10. Greenwood Press produced the major microfiche hearings file. CIS, Inc. took over ownership of Greenwood Press in 1976.

11. Other index/microfiche sets include: *Index to Current Urban Documents*, v.1– , 1972– , Westport, CT: Greenwood Press; *State Publications Index*, v.1– , 1976– , Englewood, CO: Information Handling Services.

12. See: Rebekah M. Harleston and Carla J. Stoffle, *Administration of Government Documents Collections* (Littleton, CO: Libraries Unlimited, 1974).

13. Ed Herman, "Directory of Government Document Dealers and Jobbers, 1979," *Documents to the People (DttP)* 7 (July 1979): 159–163.

14. For membership information write: Documents Expediter, Documents Expediting Project, Exchange and Gift Division, Library of Congress, Washington, DC 20540.

15. For example, see: United Nations, Secretariat, *Instructions for*

Depository Libraries Receiving United Nations Material (ST/LIB/13/Rev. 4), 9 January 1981, Annex I, 2; U.S. Government Printing Office, *Instructions to Depository Libraries* (GP 3.26: D 44/977), Nov. 1977, 7.

16. Jimmie Hoover, "Quo Vadis — The Bound Document?" *Reference Services Review* 9:3 (1981): 85--90.

17. In 1980, G.P.O. distributed over 23,000 titles in microfiche. Certain United Nations series are available in microfiche from the United States or from UNIFO Publishers, Inc. For future expansion of the U.N. microfiche program see: Luciana Marulli-Koenig, "The Dag Hammarskjold Library and United Nations Microforms," *Microform Review* 9 (Fall 1980): 236--242.

18. A list of periodicals indexed and abstracted in the *American Statistics Index* is available from the Congressional Information Service, Inc.: *Periodicals and Sources: A List of Federal Statistical Periodicals and Their Issuing Sources*.

19. As noted earlier, United Nations publications are available in microfiche. U.S. state microform publications are available from many state agencies as well as from Information Handling Services via the *State Publications Index* system. U.S. local government publications are available from Greenwood Press via the *Index to Current Urban Documents* system. Many sources of microform exist for various international and non-governmental organizations.

20. U.S., National Commission on Libraries and Information Science, *Government Publications: Their Role in the National Program for Library and Information Services*, by Bernard M. Fry (Washington, DC: Government Printing Office, 1978), 1.

21. Numerous promotional or current awareness ideas may be found in articles in *Government Publications Review, Documents to the People (DttP)*, and *Public Documents Highlights*.

22. Elizabeth A. McBride and Mary L. Morgan, "Guide to the Indexing of U.S. Government Periodicals," *Special Libraries* 67 (February 1976): 76–83; Rebekah Harleston and Carla J. Stoffle, "Government Periodicals: Seven Years Later," *Government Publications Review* 2 (1975): 323–343.

23. Judy H. Myers and Helen H. Britton, "Government Documents

in the Public Card Catalog: The Iceberg Surfaces," *Government Publications Review* 5 (1978): 311–314.

24. "Citation Indexes" refers to the various indexing services provided by the Institute for Scientific Information: *Arts and Humanities Citation Index, Social Sciences Citation Index*, and *Science Citation Index*.

25. The availability of all government publications records in convenient machine-readable form may one day allow enhanced access to government titles by merging the bibliographic records of government publications with those of general library materials. Trinity University in San Antonio is currently completing a project in which it has merged the GPO MARC records from the *Monthly Catalog of United States Government Publications* with its other machine-readable library records.

26. Charles R. McClure, "Indexing U.S. Government Periodicals: Analysis and Comments," *Government Publications Review* 5 (1978): 419.

27. Peter Hernon, *Use of Government Publications by Social Scientists* (Norwood, NJ: Ablex Publishing Corp., 1979), 62.

28. McClure, "Indexing U.S. Government Periodicals . . . ," 412–413.

LITTLE MAGAZINES IN SPECIAL COLLECTIONS AND RARE BOOK DEPARTMENTS*

Cristine C. Rom

Bizarre, astonishing, shocking! That was how the then conservative Chicago *Dial* characterized the upstart magazine *Poetry*.[1] The appearance of Harriet Monroe's *Poetry: A Magazine of Verse* in 1912 was the first clarion call of a burgeoning literary renaissance in this country and marked the beginning of a publishing revolt against establishment literature. Since the early twentieth century, little magazines have defiantly fought for innovative literature and have been the first to publish the majority of our important writers, artists, and critics. Ezra Pound, William Faulkner, e.e. cummings, James Joyce, Ernest Hemingway, T.S. Eliot, Allen Ginsberg, Jack Kerouac and Diane DiPrima are only a sampling of those well-known writers who found early acceptance in these publications.

Little magazines have also sponsored or introduced all of this century's literary trends including imagism, dadaism, surrealism, symbolism, and concrete poetry. Socialism, psychoanalysis, and Marxism were among the social movements first seriously discussed and debated by littlemag editors and writers. Little magazines provide an essential key to understanding the wealth and variety of twentieth century English-language literature, and this tradition of experimentation and innovation has continued into the 1980's.

In 1942 Alan Swallow described four main functions of little magazines: to introduce new talent, to give a voice to experimentation in literature, to foster cultural awareness, and to publish good — at times even great — literature.[2] Two more functions should be added to Swallow's list. First, littlemags present an exciting alternative in form as well as content to the established magazines with their safe and marketable literary fare. Second, they present literature from a variety of perspectives. Often in the past, such perspectives

---

*An earlier version of this essay appeared in *Credences*, Spring 1981. A special thank you to Alan J. Rocke of Case Western University, James P. Danky of the State Historical Society of Wisconsin, and the staff of the University of Wisconsin Memorial Library.

centered around regional and political differences; but the editors and writers (like members of the literary establishment) were white, middle class, and male. More recently, little magazines have given expression to the writings of previously silent segments of American society; since the mid-1960s, there has been an explosion of publishing aimed at special groups such as lesbians and gays, Afro-Americans, Chicanos, feminists, and Native Americans. Little magazines also provide good reading at very modest subscription prices; most yearly subscriptions cost less than $10.00.

Little magazines are those periodicals which exist primarily to publish material not acceptable — not profitable — to bigger, establishment publications. Characterized by their non-commercial attitudes and their penchant for the avant garde and experimental, little magazines have consistently rebelled against established literary expression and style and have demonstrated an aggressive receptivity to new authors, new ideas, and new styles. The essence of the little magazine is its experimental nature and defiant spirit. Most authorities use "little magazine" to refer exclusively to literary periodicals published in English during the twentieth century, although the adjective "literary" is often liberally interpeted. These small circulation magazines publish on the order of several hundred, or at most a couple thousand, copies per issue.

As non-commercial ventures, little magazines simply are not in the business of making money. Few editors break even; fewer still realize a profit. A 1974 National Endowment for the Arts survey of 160 United States little magazine editors indicated that approximately 75 percent incurred deficits during the previous year; accelerated inflation and rising postal rates in the last half of the 1970s have undoubtedly increased the percent of magazines working with deficits. Further, those editors surveyed stated that if they could turn a profit, that money would be used to pay contributors or be poured back into the magazine either to publish more special issues or to improve the production quality or the magazine's distribution.[3]

At best, littlemags have a tenuous financial base, and most manage to exist only because editors are willing to dig into their pockets. Low subscription rates (predicated on a belief in good literature at small expense to the reading public) and inadequate subscription and single copy sales do not cover production costs. Parenthetically, most little magazines cannot pay their contributors except in copy.

Patrons are hard to find, and grants from state and federal arts councils and private foundations really assist only a fraction of the littlemags currently publishing. Moreover, grants have generated (along with money) a storm of controversy ranging from specific complaints about magazine eligibility, the selection process, and the qualifications and biases of the moneygivers to broader questions about grants' effects on literature. Editors have aligned themselves with respect to these questions, and the controversy surfaces often in little magazines. Long-time critic of government grants Richard Kostelanetz devoted an entire issue of his *Precisely* to "Grants and the future of literature."[4] Many editors worry that grants keep littlemags alive beyond their liveliness and dictate the fashions of literature, a view cogently considered by Felix Stefanile in *Tri-Quarterly*'s special issue, "The little magazine in America."[5] Such arguments may be academic as the Reagan ax looms large over the National Endowment for the Arts.

Little magazine editors and staff are frequently also poets and writers. The 1974 NEA survey found that 60 percent of little magazines have a staff of three or less; explicitly cooperative ventures, such as most feminist magazines, usually have larger staffs.[6] They publish their magazines for pleasure, not profit, and the editor and staff invariably have regular jobs to support themselves and their literary habits, working on their literary magazine at night, on weekends, or whenever time permits. Consequently, the publication is a very personal venture and usually reflects the literary tastes of the staff, which some editors such as Ted Kooser of *Blue hotel* readily acknowledge.

Moreover, the little magazine's publishing schedule and mailing address reflect changes in the editor's life; the magazine is produced during the editor's spare time which fluctuates according to family, work, money, and health pressures. It's not unusual for a magazine to suspend publication temporarily; Seattle's *Experiment* is one extreme example, beginning in 1944 and suspending publication between 1961–1974. Naturally, most magazines move with their editors. Some move frequently, such as *Creative Review* which was published in six different cities between 1960 and 1970; an occasional magazine changes its mailing address with almost every issue.

Little magazines are experimental in the writing and art they print, but this attitude is reflected in other ways. The magazine's "packaging" can vary with each issue. Aside from the standard format, the issue may be a wall-sized poster (*Unspeakable Visions of the Individual*, vol. 6), sheaves of manila envelopes held together by nuts and bolts (*Fluxus1*), cassettes, (*Black Box*), and a box or a can (*soma-haoma*, no. 5). Additionally, little magazines may be matchbook-sized or quite large. Some magazines, for example Morris Edelson's *Quixote*, intentionally avoid a consistent size or format. They may also be unnumbered or eccentrically numbered, such as Toronto's *Ganglia*. Fortunately, most are consecutively numbered, although misnumberings do frequently occur.

These periodicals are also characterized by numerous title changes, and a few change their name with every issue. The *Once*

Series from Brightlingsea, England appeared under the following titles: *Once, Twice, Thrice, Thrice and ½, Frice, Vice, Spice, Slice, Nice*, and lastly *Ice*; each bore the subtitle *A One Shot Magazine*.

Their poor financial base; the small staffs and at-home production; and changes in format, title, and location; and the haphazard billing procedures of some editors all but insure the littlemag's short life. The average life of these publications is less than eight years, and many die after printing only one or two issues. It is not unusual, in fact, for a magazine to die a lingering death before producing a first issue; many more magazines are announced than actually begin. Some magazines, such as the aptly named *One Shot Review* and Chris Halla's *Noon at Night*, were intended to be one issue experiments. Tom Montag has suggested that first issues are generally mo. exciting, and so, perhaps short-lived magazines should not be mourned too much.[7]

From their beginnings at the turn of the century, little magazines have found their way into large libraries, especially research libraries. Acquired in a more or less haphazard manner, these magazines tended to be the better known littles, like *Kenyon Review* and *Prairie Schooner*, with traditional formats. In the past, they were processed in the standard library manner, bound in library buckram, and shelved in the general library stacks. With the recognition by the academic community of little magazines as unique and important literary publications, and especially after Frederick Hoffman published *The Little Magazine: A History and Bibliography* in 1947, special collection and rare book departments took up the task of acquiring and housing these periodicals.

These departments are best able to purchase difficult-to-handle materials, to pull together related materials already in the library, and to protect them from the ravages of open shelf use; in effect, these departments may design their procedures to accommodate the most unusual and eccentric aspects of little magazine publishing.

Armed with an understanding of the spirit and nature of little magazines and their role in American cultural and intellectual history, librarians are prepared, in Tom Montag's words, to "stalk the little magazine."[8] The plethora of little magazines and the time-consuming job of locating and ordering them necessitate a manageable collection policy; few libraries, like the University of Wisconsin-Madison, are able to acquire comprehensively. State, regional, or special focus little magazines would comprise a viable and cohesive collection that the department staff could learn intimately and service knowledgeably and efficiently. Whatever the collecting policy, the department will also want to subscribe to a selection of basic news and review little magazines as well as several magazines outside the collection's scope for comparison and evaluation.

Only a fraction of little magazines are critically reviewed in library periodicals. Bill Katz has long been an enthusiast of this publishing genre and perceptively and sympathetically reviews little magazines in his *Library Journal* column. Better known veteran magazines (e.g., *Dacotah Territory, Montana Gothic*) are also listed in his *Magazines for Libraries*, but the indexing information found here is seldom complete, and the mailing address and subscription prices are often out of date. The quarterly *Serials Review* regularly publishes a column of 10–25 little magazine reviews; special focus columns are alternated with miscellaneous reviews. *Serials Review* annotations provide complete ordering information, the original place of publication, and previous titles; they average 500 words and are written by knowledgeable editors, writers, and librarians. Still, these two periodicals can consider only a small portion of titles annually. This frustrating circumstance is somewhat ameliorated by several dedicated small press publishers and little magazine editors, and the best sources for information on new titles are other little magazines.

The most important source of information for a large number of little magazines is Len Fulton and Ellen Ferber's *International Directory of Little Magazines and Small Presses* which has been issued annually since 1965 by Dustbooks. Fulton's directory (often simply referred to as the "Dust directory") is the only work of its kind, and the most recent 1981/82 edition lists over 3,000 presses and magazines. The directory is designed to serve writers, editors, and librarians. The main section is an alphabetical listing of magazines and presses. Each magazine citation includes the publication's title and subtitle; press name and editor; current mailing address and subscription price; anticipated publishing frequency for the current and next years and the number of issues published during the previous year; beginning date; circulation figures and average number and size of pages; description of the contents and sometimes a list of recent contributors; and subject emphasis. Moreover, the recent directory has expanded subject and regional indices (now including foreign countries) as well as a list of some 200 little magazine and small press distributors.

The "Dust directory" is essential for anyone involved in little magazine and small press writing, publishing, and collecting. However, it must be noted that Fulton interprets "little magazine" rather liberally, and his directory also includes alternative lifestyle magazines, comics, undergrounds, fanzines, sci-fi rags, and small academic journals. The directory, although international in scope, favors American publications; the *British Directory* of little magazines and small presses (begun in 1974/75) is similar in content and intent to Fulton's work. Dustbooks publishes two complementary directories:

Small Press Record of Books in Print and *Directory of Small Magazine Press Editors and Publishers*.

Fulton and Ferber also publish *Small Press Review*, which appears monthly and updates their annual directory. A "New listings" column in each issue prints directory format entries for new titles; "News and notes" and "Feedback" keep readers abreast of magazine address changes, contests, readings, conferences, title cessations, and calls for manuscripts. Reading requests for manuscripts is an important way of learning about new little magazines, eager to fill their literary coffers, and special theme issues. In addition, *Small Press Review* publishes articles of interest to littlemag editors and small press people, occasionally prints bibliographies of twentieth century authors, and reviews small press books, and, less frequently, little magazines. Additional information can be culled from ads and the SPRMart.

In 1978 Fulton's magazine began carrying the Small Press Book Club selection lists (which includes individual little magazine issues of special note) and order forms. The writing is lively and informed, and the reviews are knowledgeable. In June 1981 *Small Press Review* published a special issue on little magazines and small press publications and libraries with a range of articles by knowledgeable writers. With the demise of Montag's *Margins* in 1976, *Small Press Review* is now the most important clearinghouse of little magazine and small press information.

Northeast Rising Sun is similar to *Small Press Review* and publishes 10-20 short reviews in each issue, which, unfortunately, are often confusingly scattered among the magazine's graphics and advertisements; it also prints articles, interviews and news. *Brick: A Journal of Reviews* focuses on Canadian publishers and writers and pays particular, but not exclusive, attention to small press publishing and also prints articles and criticism.

The *Literary Monitor: The Voice of Contemporary Literature* is a bi-monthly tabloid publishing several hundred reviews of littlemags and small press publications annually. "Mini-reviews" of such notable magazines as *Bachy* are mixed with extended criticism. The *Monitor* also publishes articles, photos, interviews, letters, news, lists of new publications, and an extensive list of books and magazines received. *Happiness Holding Tank* publishes far fewer reviews but generally contains a mountain of valuable information; issues list new titles, dead magazines, requests for manuscripts, and poetry contests. It also publishes poetry, essays, criticism, and news items.

Motherroot Journal: A Women's Review of Small Presses reviews small press books by, about, and of special interest to women, and most issues contain some magazine reviews. A large number of the reviewers are also writers and editors. Reviews are lengthy and informative and skillfully put the material into a feminist perspective. *Motherroot Journal* also publishes essays, interviews, and news as well as announcements of awards and ads for feminist presses, bookstores, and magazines. This little magazine is a folded tabloid similar to Diane Kruchkow's *Stony Hills* and ranks with Fulton's excellent *Small Press Review*. Joan Polly and Andrea Chesman's *Guide to Women's Publishing* is another excellent source for information about women's littlemags; its annotations are very good, and the list of feminist bookstores will help librarians trying to track down new titles.

Sipapu, according to its editor Noel Peattie, is a "newsletter for librarians, editors, collectors, and others interested in Third World Studies, the counterculture, the alternative (formerly underground) and independent (also called small) presses." Reviews are found among interviews and articles. The magazine is weighted toward alternative magazines but gives enough consideration to littlemags to warrant reading. It's a lively magazine, and Peattie is a serious student of the field.

The Committee of Small Magazine Editors and Publishers, COSMEP, publishes a six to ten page monthly newsletter of news and notes of interest to its members, including announcements of contests, lists of new titles, reviews, occasional essays, business, and letters. The manuscript request section is quite useful, although complete mailing addresses are not always given. Subscriptions to the newly renamed newsletter, *The Independent Publisher*, are by membership.

Several local COSMEP groups also publish newsletters. *Coda: Poets and Writers Newsletter* is 30–40 pages of articles, photos, news; announcements of contests, grants, and awards; personal jottings and advertisements. The articles are detailed and cover all areas of interest to writers. Past articles have included "Agents and Authors: Both Sides Are Right" and "Movie Writing," and the June/July 1976 issue had a lengthy article on little magazines in libraries. *Coda*'s bias is toward better known writers and veteran magazines but is, nonetheless, valuable. The Coordinating Council of Literary Magazines also publishes a newsletter detailing grant information and listing recipients with full mailing data. Since certain editors, such as Felix Stefanile of *Sparrow Poverty Pamphlets*, are not willing to play the grant "game," and many excellent magazines never receive CCLM monies, the range of titles listed here is limited. Despite this limitation, the *CCLM Newsletter* can still be useful.

Stony Hills: The New England Alternative Press Review is a tabloid packed with ads and reviews of small press books and littlemags by regional authors, about New England, or published in New England. All contributors are well-known writers and editors, and the reviews are in-depth, well written, and lively with a generous sampling of the material under consideration. *Stony Hills* also contains interviews, photographs, news, articles, and occasional bibliographies of regional publications; for example, vol. 1 no. 1 listed all small presses and little magazines in Massachusetts.

Many local poetry groups publish newsletters, and the Long Island Poetry Collective's *Newsletter* is a good example from an area of much literary activity. The production is less than slick and not always easy to read, but the *Newsletter* features much information: four to ten reviews, a calendar of New York City area literary events, a small press markets section, and much data on new titles and magazines calling for manuscripts. Hundreds of such local newsletters are published around the country, but they vary greatly in scope and quality. Some bookstore(s), such as Two Hands in Chicago, also put out newsletters. Lastly, most little magazines print lists of other magazines received on exchange, requests for manuscripts, advertisements, and recommended magazines. These should not be ignored and, for special interest littlemags (especially gay/lesbian and Native American ones) are often the best places to locate similar magazines.

Because little magazine editors move frequently (and some leave no forwarding address), it is imperative to place subscription orders as quickly as possible. Locating the publisher — most littles are ordered directly from the editor — is the most common difficulty in little magazine acquisitions, but this can usually be avoided by prompt ordering. Some address changes show up in *Small Press Review* and the *Cosmep Newsletter*. Writers and Poets, Inc., which produces *Coda*, is usually willing to help track down editors.

Other problems that may be encountered are changes in titles and numbering systems (which are more confusing than problematic) and editors who will not accept subscriptions but prefer single copy orders. Although billing procedures are not as universally eccentric as they once were, some editors still have informal billing procedures, and this is an obvious snag for the red tape of library triplicate billing. Department staff will have to develop procedures that suit the library without frustrating the editor. Also, some editors may not be able to send all of the issues ordered; often, the number of copies printed varies from issue to issue, and editors may not have a complete set of back issues to sell.

These are, however, all rather minor problems and are often easily settled by a personal letter to the editor. In fact, Tom Montag, himself an editor, believes that editors are best dealt with on a personal basis.[9] One of the notable benefits of having a little magazine collection in a rare book or special collection department is flexibility; librarians, aware of the informality and unusual aspects of ordering little magazines, can adjust their procedures to smooth this bureaucratic process for themselves and the editors.

Back issues are not always available from the editor, and most librarians will find it necessary to pick up individual issues on the out-of-print market. Robert Wilson's Phoenix Bookshop (New York, New York), Sand Dollar Books (Albany, California), Asphodel Bookstore (Burton, Ohio), Casa Editorial (San Francisco, California), and Harold A. Landry (London, England) are a few dealers specializing in rare and out-of-print literary magazines. Landry offers mostly complete sets of classics at steep prices; Wilson is particularly good for individual copies of early twentieth century and beat generation magazines; and Asphodel is best for single copies of recent American littles.

The importance of ordering quickly cannot be over emphasized. With the increased interest in these ephemeral publications, issues listed in these dealers' catalogs sell quickly. For early twentieth century magazines, it is becoming increasingly difficult to buy complete sets and, in some cases, individual copies. Some dealer's catalogs, particularly Landry's, are valuable reference sources.

A large number of little magazines have been reprinted, primarily by Kraus-Thomson Press but also by Johnson Press, Cass Press, and several smaller reprint and microform companies; some current titles are now available from University Microforms International. Kraus-Thomson's reprint catalogs, in particular, are extremely useful reference sources containing important bibliographic and descriptive data.

Two other acquisition methods deserve mention. It can be profitable to visit local, independent bookstores; they are often good places to find regional or special interest littlemags. Similarly, small press distribution services — such as NESPA, Bookslinger, COSMEP, and Plains Distribution — may be more convenient for smaller collections. Their selections and ordering policies differ significantly. The sixteenth edition of the "Dust directory" has an extensive list of distributors, and *Cosmep Newsletter* occasionally carries up-to-date distribution information. Requests for catalogs and ordering information should be addressed to individual services.

The processing and cataloging of these periodicals may be the two most difficult and crucial aspects of little magazine collecting — difficult because the librarian will have to develop new procedures best suited to the eccentricities of these ephemera while still working within the existing library framework, and crucial because these two tasks so directly affect reference service. In all honesty, the little magazine librarian may discover that not all library staff members will understand why these ephemeral materials should be collected or given full cataloging, and the oddities of little magazine publishing could easily change this lack of understanding into a strong dislike.

Moreover, to insure proper handling of each item and for the sake of intralibrary relations, the processing and cataloging should be done by the department housing the collection; this also gives the staff familiarity with the material, directly affecting the quality of reference service.

It is essential that the department servicing the collection have accurate kardex and card catalog records regardless whether the magazines are recorded elsewhere in the library. The dearth of published comprehensive bibliographies means that the kardex file is the department's best reference source. Each title should have the following information noted on its kardex card: title and subtitle; press and editor's name; current mailing address and subscription price; first and all subsequent places of publication in chronological order; all variant titles and subtitles and cross reference notes; complete numbering data; where the magazine is indexed; sister publications; variant, damaged, and missing issue information; billing notes; indications of analytics for the card catalog; and notes about superseding, suspension, cessations, and mergers.

Any other useful information such as references to books and articles about the magazine, subject emphasis, guest editors, publishing frequency, claim notes, comments from the editor, or inclusion in the "Dust directory" may also be written on the kardex record. For insurance purposes, it may prove helpful to write the current market value of the titles found in out-of-print catalogs. Most of this information is readily available to the staff member ordering, checking in, and cataloging the issues, but much of it is lost if not recorded at the time. A well-maintained, accurate, and detailed kardex is the key to a little magazine collection.

The necessity for thorough and accurate cataloging of little magazines cannot be overemphasized, and the content and format of the cataloging outlined below are best for properly identifying each title, and at the same time, are flexible enough to account for the extremely complicated bibliography of little magazines. The basic catalog record should contain the magazine's full title, the beginning and ending volume, number, and date, and the original place of publication. All additional identifying information should be put in a dropped note. For the majority of incoming magazines, this basic information can be found on each issue. For the remainder, the cataloger will have to rely on the department's records and holdings, published reference books, and correspondence with editors and other libraries collecting littlemags.

The identification of a little magazine's title is not always a straightforward task because of frequent and unpredictable title changes. The change may be drastic or slight, permanent or temporary. Although each case should be evaluated separately, several basic guidelines will prove helpful. For simple title changes, provide new cataloging for *each* different title, including a supersedes/superseded note on the kardex and catalog cards. Often a new name is accompanied by a new numbering system, but in any case, record the numbering as it appears on the newly renamed title. For example, *Berkeley Samisdat* changed its name in 1974 to *Samisdat* but maintained its numbering. The revised cards for the later title should indicate that it supersedes and continues the numbering of the former, and the records for *Berkeley Samisdat* should indicate that it was superseded and continued by *Samisdat*. Both titles should have catalog and kardex cards.

For magazines whose titles vary occasionally, merely note variant titles on the kardex and catalog cards in a dropped note and provide cross references in both files. One example is *Poor Old Tired Horse*; number 22 was entitled *Poth*, number 23 *Teapoth*, and number 24 returned to the original title. It is most logical to catalog this magazine under *Poor Old Tired Horse* and provide references from the other two titles. If the title changes with most issues as with *Once, Twice, Thrice, Thrice and ½*, etc., catalog the magazine under the first or most appropriate series title and make references from all other titles for the kardex and card catalog. The numbering and publishing information for each issue may not be the same; record what is found on the issues, noting additional interpretive information as needed.

As a further complication, cover and inside titles may also vary. Most often, the cover title reflects the contents of a special monographic issue, such as issue 7/8 of *Rockbottom* which was entitled *First-Person Intense: A Prose Anthology*. The magazine's title and number were on the verso of the title page, and it is likely that readers will only remember the issue title rather than the magazine's title. Make author and title analytics for such issues and note this on the kardex. This situation does not constitute a title change. Occasionally, however, there may be no logical reason for the differences between cover and inside titles; they are merely variants. *Surrealist Transformaction*, for example, appeared on the inside of all issues, but two variant titles, *Transformation* and *Transformaction*, appeared on some of the issues' covers. Such magazines should be cataloged under the most consistently used title, in this case *Surrealist Transformaction*, with cross references provided from the variant titles; notes should be added also to the catalog and kardex cards.

A rare magazine may arrive without a title or with it cleverly hidden in the cover design or secreted inside the text; here the problem is more of identification, not cataloging, and familiarity with the collection and publishers' habits is the only way to solve the puzzle. Conscientious maintenance of a little magazine collection requires frequent recataloging and revising of kardex records, some imagination, and a lot of flexibility, but the time spent on these activities will be invaluable to staff and patrons.

A title can reflect a magazine's personality, and the capitalization and punctuation on the catalog card should reflect that found on the magazine. Moreover, since subtitles change more frequently than titles, they should not be included in the title statement but put in a note. Lastly, little magazine titles are wonderful and interesting, a few novel names are: *Urbane Gorilla, If Grandma Had Balls She'd Be Grandpa, Spirit That Moves Us, hanging loose, Plucked Chicken*, and *Loose Lips Sink Ships*.

The main body of the catalog card should properly identify the beginning and ending volume, number, and date and the original place of publication. Many magazines have identical or similar titles; at least five have been named *Folio*, and four *Contact* (not counting *Contact II* or those spelled *Contac*). Even unusual names are often duplicated; there have been three entitled *i.e.* and two called *Hippocrene*. The best way to distinguish between identical titles is by their publication dates and first place of publication, and this format is in agreement with AACR II. The numbering used on the catalog card should match that used by the magazine — volume, cycle, series, phase, etc. — and varying publication places should be listed in chronological order in a dropped note.

If the necessary information cannot be determined from issues in the collection, the cataloger should check the recently published *Catalog of Little Magazines* for titles held in the University of Wisconsin's Rare Book Department. It contains entries for more than 3,000 English-language twentieth century littles acquired before October 1977; an addendum adds titles acquired between November 1977 and June 1979. The entries include the magazine's title, subtitle, and variant titles; original place of publication and name of the press; ISSN and LCCN; and holdings in the Rare Book Department. Cross references from most variant titles and some general notes are provided; university-sponsored magazines have additional references from the sponsoring institutions. The University of Wisconsin-Madison's collection is one of the best of its kind, and this printed catalog has few errors or lacunae. The *International Directory of Little Magazines and Small Presses* and *Small Press Review* can also be very helpful in locating publishing information. Hoffman's *The Little Magazine*, out-of-print and reprint catalogs, and the *Union List of Little Magazines* are most helpful for older titles; *TriQuarterly*'s *The Little Magazine in America* is good for "big" little magazines from the 1940s to the mid-1970s, and *Ulrich's* lists many current little magazines. Since *New Serial Titles* and the Union List of Magazines record only library holdings and not necessarily complete publishing data, they are limited in value. OCLC is also limited because of the difficulty of searching titles such as *A, Z, X*, and *Poetry*. Little magazines indices, like the Kraus-Thomson set, often provide useful bibliographic information.

Libraries collecting littlemags are generally very willing to share information and exchange catalog records. A descriptive list of these libraries appeared in "Poetry in the Hothouse" in the June/July 1976 issue of *Coda*. As a last resort, the cataloger may want to write the editor; they do not always remember where and when their magazine began, but they are generally glad to help. Many editors' addresses are listed in the *Directory of American Fiction Writers*, the *Directory of American Poets*, and Fulton's *Directory of Small Magazine Press Editors*. Any information useful in identifying a specific title should be recorded in a note on both catalog and kardex cards. This usually includes: differing titles for which new cataloging is not provided, subtitles, chronological listing of places of publication, and supersedes notes. Other pertinent data include statements about the magazine's significance (e.g., contains the first publication of a now-famous writer), suspension notes, editorships, format, provenance, and relationships to other magazines.

A significant portion of little magazines publish monographic issues, and this format is increasing in popularity; for some magazines, like *Wolfsong*, single-author issues are the rule. It is important to provide author/title analytics for these issues. Moreover, since many littlemags occasionally produce single focus issues (e.g., contemporary French poetry in translation, Beat Generation memoirs, or baseball and poetry), it is beneficial to provide subject and/or title access. A detailed discussion of subject cataloging by Sanford Berman, entitled "Access to Alternatives," appeared in a special issue of *Collection Building* devoted to alternative materials and libraries.[10]

To protect the issues from the ravages of open shelf use, little magazines should be shelved in a locked area and serviced only by library personnel; eccentric numbering, unusual formats, and the fragile condition of these materials underscore this necessity. Furthermore, a certain portion of any collection will require oversized, flat shelving, and flimsy issues will need special handling. Such procedures, unfortunately but necessarily, separate people and literature — contrary to most editors' intentions. Several services might ease this situation. Duplicates of popular titles could be located in a reading area or placed in the general library stacks; similarly, newly received and physically durable issues could be displayed in a supervised browsing area. Also, the staff could prepare briefly annotated monthly acquisition lists or weekly summaries of recent issues.

With the rare book and special collection departments' emphasis on preservation, little magazines must not be bound but rather retained in their original covers. A better solution is to store individual issues in acid-free evelopes or folders or to keep complete sets in custom-made acid-free pamboxes or portfolios. These periodicals are extremely delicate creatures which seldom age well, and the binding process accelerates deterioration.

Several other practical reasons militate against binding littlemags. Many use cheap paper not suited to binding, while others print their title and volume information only on the spine. Moreover, since each issue may differ in size and shape, it is impractical as well an uneconomical for the binder to work with them. It is, lastly, contrary to the basic function of special collection and rare book departments to alter the original state of materials. Since many little magazines are printed on low quality paper, and some are printed on newsprint, second reprint or microfilm copies of heavily used titles should be available for all but exceptional use.

The reference structure for little magazines, though improving, is still underdeveloped. Most of the reference books have been published in the last ten years, and growing interest in this unique type of publishing is welcomed by librarians and researchers.

The best history of the genre is Frederick J. Hoffman's *The Little Magazine: A History and Bibliography*; first published in 1947, it brought these magazines to the attention of the academic community. His volume contains a well written, scholarly history through the mid-1940s and a thorough bibliography of English-language little magazines. The bibliography is arranged chronologically and provides complete publishing information as well as a short description of each magazine's history, editorial policies, and noteworthy contributors. It is fairly comprehensive and accurate, especially when one considers that, at the time, there was no one major library collection at Hoffman's disposal. Hoffman's scope is international, but the work is best for American titles. A bibliography of books and articles about little magazines is appended.

Hoffman's book was an enormous and successful undertaking and has become the standard history of the genre. *The Little Magazine* is a must for the reference collection of any library collecting little magazines and is recommended for any academic or major research library.[11] The major drawback of Hoffman's book is that it ends with the 1940s, leaving more than 30 years of history and bibliography unwritten. Charles P. Silet's "Annotated Checklist of Articles and Books on American Little Magazines" is extensive and updates Hoffman. Two articles each by Fulton and Allen in *American Libraries* also help fill the gap. Reed Whittemore's slender pamphlet investigates the little magazine editors' "real and imaginary responsibilities" to larger society; he looks at *Poetry, Partisan Review, Fugitive, Southern Review*, and *Sewanee Review*. Twelve additional titles are also briefly considered, and a bibliography and a very short list of suggested reading is appended.

TriQuarterly recently published *The Little Magazine in America: A Modern Documentary History*.[12] While the volume has a wealth of essays and some are very interesting, it is not a history. The work provides no context, no sense of the growth and development of little magazines, and no assessment of contemporary trends. It makes no attempt to deal with feminist, native American, or lesbian/gay magazines which are important recent developments in alternative publishing. This hefty volume contains several original and insightful essays (particularly those by Fulton, Montag, Creeley, and Stefanile) and reprints informative articles by editors of well-known magazines. However, the text and bibliography are much too heavily biased in favor of big-established little magazines, and the bibliography is poor, as the editors made no attempt to check which titles were indexed in the obvious little magazine indexes. Still, the scarcity of historical material makes *TriQuarterly*'s flawed work a recommended acquisition for the reference collection.

Many early little magazine editors — including Harriet Monroe (*Poetry*), Margaret Anderson (*Little Review*), and Alfred Kreymborg (*Glebe* and *Others*) — wrote bibliographies giving personal assessments of their magazines' struggles and achievements; these are also entertaining accounts of the intellectual milieu. There are, too, a growing number of published histories on individual magazines, like Dougald McMillan's *Transition: The History of a Literary Era, 1927–1938* and Milton Reigelman's *The Midland: A Venture in Literary Regionalism*. Several general intellectual histories, such as Daniel Aaron's *Writers on the Left* and James B. Gilbert's *Writers and Partisans*, provide good contextual analysis of little magazines. Jackson Bryer's "A Trial-Track for Racers: Margaret Anderson and the *Little Review*" (1965) and Morris Edelson's "Six Little Magazines" (1973) are only two examples of doctoral dissertations in the area.[13]

Much recent little magazine history is not yet in books but found in other little magazines. *Galley: The Little Magazine for Little Magazine Publishers* (1949–1953) contains much of historical interest. Number one was a little magazine directory, number three a who's who in little magazine publishing, and number four a compilation of little magazine presses. *Trace: A Chronicle of Living Literature* (1952–1972) published an annual directory of English-language poetry and small literary magazines from all over the world. Warren French's article on little magazines of the 1950s appeared in *College English* in 1961.

Margins: A Review of Little Mags and Small Press Books, which published from 1972–1976, is an excellent repository of literature and little magazine information. Special issues focused on topics ranging from native American writng to the role of the reviewer and "Women, Poetry, and the Small Presses." The essence of *Margins*, however, was its reviews. The recently defunct *Poetry Information* (1970-1979/80) was a gold mine of information about British titles; it also printed good reviews of American literary magazines.

Small Press Review is a good chronicle of developments since the mid-1960s, and Fulton's introduction to the 1980/81 "Dust Directory" is a brief synopsis of significant trends in little magazine and small press publishing during the last two decades. Historical articles are published by many littlemags, and a department card file is the best way to keep track of them.

Since 1900, at least 4,000 English-language little magazines have been published, and many of them lack tables of contents, indexes, and lists of contributors. Not surprisingly, one of the most challenging task facing the little magazine librarian is locating specific works by specific authors. Fortunately, several published indexes mitigate this problem.

The best index, in terms of the number of magazines and the time covered, is the *Comprehensive Index to English-Language Little Magazines, 1890-1970* edited by Marion Sader of Kraus-Thomson Press. Series one is an eight-volume author index to 100 well-known English and American titles. The author names are standardized and verified, and ample cross references from variant names and pseudonyms are provided. Book and film reviews are included. The index, with over 2,000,000 entries, is accurate and carefully prepared; the typography is clean, and the format easy to use. Complete bibliographic information is given for each entry and includes: author, title, and translator (when appropriate); type of article (e.g., prose, review, photograph); and the pages, title, volumes, and date of the magazine.

The major flaw of this index is that it provides no access by title or subject (other than personal name), and this severely limits its general usefulness for non-specialists. Yet, it is the best and most complete little magazine index available and is recommended for all research libraries. Kraus-Thomson has reprinted most titles indexed in series one. Series two is still in the planning stages and will index another 100 titles.

Since the duplication is minimal, librarians may find other special and general indexes helpful. The now defunct series, *Index to American Little Magazines, Index to Commonwealth Little Magazines*, and *Index to Little Magazines*, provide author, title, and subject indexing to a large number of titles. Unfortunately, none is as accurate as the Kraus-Thomson set, and there is no consistency from one volume to the next in titles selected for inclusion. Bloomfield's *Author Index to Selected British Little Magazines, 1930-1939* and Leverette's

Index to Little Magazines of Ontario, 1968-1973 are more specific and very limited in their focus.

Access Index to Little Magazines, first published in 1977, annually indexes 74 currently publishing American titles selected by Len Fulton. Each volume has a separate author, title, and subject index, and each citation includes: author, title, and name of the magazine; pages, volume, number, and date; and the type of material. The author section indexes all material; the title section indexes only fiction and poetry; and the subject section indexes only nonfiction. It is a significant omission that the title index does not include nonfiction works. However, the index is easy to use, and the selection of magazines is broad, representing the wide range of the genre in this country.

Two general magazine indexes, *American Humanities Index* and *Index of American Periodical Verse*, also include current little magazines and are accurate and easy to use; the Alternative Press Index is marginally helpful. Many little magazines, such as *Sipapu*, are self-indexed, and some magazines like *Serif* publish indexes and histories of other notable little mags. The well-staffed department may want to provide an in-house indexing service. Alternatively, a card file indicating what little magazines are indexed, where, and for which years may prove the best use of these published indexes.

Reference needs will vary according to the size and scope of each collection. Regular perusal of the basic news and review little magazines is essential to keep the staff abreast of current trends and topics of import to editors and writers. Moreover, familiarity with the individual collection and an understanding of the history and contemporary context of today's little magazines are invaluable in meeting these varying reference needs. The staff will soon discover, however, that many questions cannot be adequately answered by these few magazines nor by the meager selection of published histories, bibliographies, and indexes. Department files need to fill the void, and these should be developed to meet specific patron demands. Several in-house files have already been suggested — author/title and subject analytics, an index of contributors appearing in littlemags held in the collection, annotated acquisition lists, and a card file of books and articles about the history of the little magazine movement and individual titles.

One particularly useful file records interviews appearing in the department's little magazines. The University of Wisconsin-Madison, for instance, has indexed interviews in all issues received since 1975; this file, which is part of the public card catalog, now has over 1,000 interviews. Besides containing the expected information about the person's life and work, formative influences, and the craft of their art, many interviews also include bibliographies and chronologies.

Other useful files might include subject bibliographies, an index to little magazine small presses and descriptions of their other publications, an editor index, and an index to reviews of magazines held in the collection. Many littlemag readers are also writers themselves, and a calendar of deadlines for contest and grant submissions and of conferences and small press book fairs will undoubtedly be appreciated. Since photographs of artists and writers are difficult to locate, such a file could prove valuable; similarly, art work is not well covered by published indexes but should be available to patrons.

Lists of distribution services and bookstores specializing in little magazines and small press publications will find good use as well as descriptions of other little magazine collections. Little magazine advertisements and ephemera often contain much hard-to-locate information, and correspondence with editor, writers, and publishers is a unique reference source. Such department files are perhaps the most persuasive argument for housing little magazines in special collection and rare book departments.

Little magazines, since their beginnings over 70 years ago, have been the vanguard of twentieth century thought and literary expression; the beginning of many careers and literary movements can be found in these unique periodicals. Little magazines continue into the 1980s to search for the best contemporary literature, and they still provide the best publishing opportunity for unknown writers and artists. No longer is it sufficient for only a few major libraries to collect these magazines and merely store them for future historical research. All libraries must ultimately consider littlemags for their collections. Special collection and rare book departments are most suited to acquiring, cataloging, and housing these magazines and can provide the best service to researchers, editors and writers, and most importantly, all literature enthusiasts.

NOTES

1. Daniel J. Cahill, *Harriet Monroe* (New York: Twayne Publishers), 1973, p. 76.

2. Alan Swallow, "The Little Magazines," *Prairie Schooner* 16 (Winter 1942), pp. 238–43.

3. "The Economics of Little Magazines: A Report from Leonard Randolph and the Literature Program of the National Endowment for the Arts," *Margins* 17 (February 1975), p. 9.

4. *Precisely: two* (1978).

5. Felix Stefanile, "The Little Magazine Today," *TriQuarterly* 43 (Fall 1978), pp. 648–663.

6. "The Economics of Little Magazines . . . " p. 11.

7. "The Economics of Little Magazines . . . " p. 66.

8. Tom Montag, "Stalking the Little Magazine," *Serials Librarian* v1 n3 (Spring 1977), pp. 281–303. This excellent article by a knowledgeable writer is available free from Montag (Box 8, Fairwater, WI 53931) to persons sending a 6 by 9 inch envelope with 52 cents postage.

9. Montag, p. 291.

10. Sanford Berman, "Access to Alternatives: New Approaches to Cataloging," *Collection Building* v2 n2 (March 1980), pp. 28–53. This special issue, "Alternative Materials in Libraries: A Handbook" was very ably edited by two authorities in the field, Elliot Shore (Temple University) and James P. Danky (State Historical Society of Wisconsin). This volume presents a persuasive case for the acquisition of alternative materials but argues that these publications should be integrated into the general library collection and not segregated in special collection and rare book departments.

11. Reprints of Hoffman's book are available from Kraus-Thomson.

12. This book was initially published as issue 43 of *TriQuarterly*; the hardback edition was published by Pushcart Press and has an index not in the magazine issue.

13. Both dissertations were written at the University of Wisconsin-Madison.

SELECTED BIBLIOGRAPHY

Allen, Charles. "Bibliography of Little Magazines," *American Libraries* 2 (January 1971), 35–47.

──────. "Little Magazines in America, 1945–1970," *American Libraries* 3 (October 1972), 964–971.

Alternative Press Index: An Index to Alternative and Radical Publications. Baltimore: Alternative Press Center, 1969– .

American Humanities Index: A Quarterly Index to Creative and Critical Journals in the Arts. Troy, NY: Whitson Pub. Co., 1976-- .

Anderson, Elliot, and Mary Kinzie, eds. *The Little Magazine in America: A Modern Documentary History.* Yonkers, NY: Pushcart Press, 1978.
This was originally published as n43 of *TriQuarterly.*

Bloomfield, Barry Cambray, ed. *Author Index to Selected British Little Magazines, 1930--1939.* London: Mansell Information, 1976.

Brick: A Journal of Reviews. 1976-- . Stan Dragland, ed. Box 219, Ilderton, Ontario N0M 2A0, Canada.

British Directory of Little Magazines and Small Presses. New Malden, England: Dustbooks, 1974-- .

Burke, John Gordon, Len Fulton, and Ned Kehde, eds. *Access Index to Little Magazines.* Syracuse, NY/Stockton, CA: Gaylord Professional Publications, 1977-- .

Coda: Poets and Writers Newsletter. 1973-- . Poets & Writers, Inc., 201 West 54th Street, New York, NY 10019.

Columbia Road Review: A Review Magazine of Southern Presses. 1980- . Kathryn E. King, ed. King Publications, P.O. Box 19332, Washington, DC 20036 (supersedes *COSMEP News South*).

Committee of Small Magazine Editors and Publishers. *The Whole COSMEP Catalog.* Paradise, CA: Dustbooks, 1973.

Directory of American Fiction Writers. New York: Poets and Writers, Inc., 1976. 1977 supplement.

Directory of American Poets. New York: Poets and Writers, Inc., 1975. 1976, 1977 supplements.

"Economics of Little Magazines: A Report from Leonard Randolph and the Literature Program of the National Endowment for the Arts," *Margins* 17 (February 1975), 4--11, 66--67.

French, Warren. "Little Magazines in the Fifties," *College English* 22 (May 1961), 547--552.

Fulton, Len. "Anima Rising, Little Magazines in the Sixties," *American Libraries* 2 (January 1971), 25--47.

Fulton, Len and Ellen Ferber, eds. *Directory of Small Magazine/ Press Editors and Publishers*. Paradise, CA: Dustbooks, 1969- .

----------------. *International Directory of Little Magazines and Small Presses*. Paradise, CA: Dustbooks, 1965-- . Originally entitled: *Directory of Little Magazines*.

Fulton, Len. "Little Magazines: Touching the Biosphere," *American Libraries* 5 (February 1974), 73--75.

Fulton, Len and Ellen Ferber, eds. *Small Press Record of Books in Print*. Paradise, CA: Dustbooks, 1969- .

Galley: The Little Magazine for Little Magazine Publishers. v1-4, n2, 1949--1953. Hollywood, CA.

Happiness Holding Tank. 1970-- . Albert Drake, ed. Stone Press, 1790 Grand River, Okemos, MI 48864.

Hoffman, Frederick J., Charles Allen and Carolyn Ulrich. *The Little Magazine: A History and Bibliography*. Princeton, NJ: Princeton University Press, 1947. (Repr. by Kraus-Thomson, 1967.)

Independent Publisher. 1969- . Richard Morris, ed. Box 703, San Francisco, CA 94101. (Supersedes *COSMEP Newsletter*.)

Index to American Little Magazines, 1900-1975. Troy, NY: Whitson Publishing Co., 1965--1974.

Index to Commonwealth Little Magazines, 1964-1975. Troy, NY: Whitson Pub. Co., 1964--1968; New York: Johnson Rpt. Co., 1968--1975.

Index to Little Magazines, 1948-1967. Denver, CO: Alan Swallow, 1949--1970.

Lever, Rachelle. *The Little Magazine in South America since 1945*. Johannesburg: University of Witwatersrand, 1973.

Leverette, Clarke E., ed. *Index to Little Magazines of Ontario, 1968-1973*. London, Ontario: Killaly Press, 1972-1975.

————————. "Pleasure of Small Literary Magazines," *Emergency Librarian*, 3 (July 1976), 16–19.

Literary Monitor: The Voice of Contemporary Literature. 1977– . Gary Lagier, ed. TLM Press, 1070 Noriega, Sunnyvale, CA 94086.

Little Magazine and Contemporary Culture. [New York] : Modern Language Association, 1966.

Margins: A Review of Little Mags and Small Press Books. n1–28/29/30, 1972–1976. Milwaukee, WI; Fair Water, WI.

Montag, Tom. *Concern/s: Essays & Reviews, 1972–1976*. Milwaukee, WI: Pentagram Press, 1977.

————————. "Stalking the Little Magazine," *Serials Librarian* v1 n3 (Spring 1977), 281–303.

Newsletter. 1974– . Long Island Poetry Collective, Box 773, Huntington, NY 11743.

Northeast Rising Sun: A Small Press Review Magazine. 1976– . Pamela Beach Plymell, ed. Cherry Valley Editions, Box 303, Cherry Valley, NY 13320.

Peattie, Noel. *The Living Z: A Guide to the Literature of the Counter-Culture, the Alternative Press, and Little Magazines*. Milwaukee, WI: Margins Press, 1975.

Poetry Information. n1–20/21, 1970–1979/80. London, England.

Polly, Joan and Andrea Chesman. *Guide to Women's Publishing*. Paradise, CA: Dustbooks, 1978. (Second edition forthcoming summer 1981.)

Roemig, Robert F., ed. *Catalog of Little Magazines*. Madison, WI: University of Wisconsin Press, 1979.

Rom, Cristine C. *Women's Writing: Feminist Little Magazines in the Rare Book Department*. Madison, WI: Memorial Library, 1978.

Sader, Marion, ed. *Comprehensive Index to English-Language Little Magazines, 1890–1970*. Milwood, NY: Kraus-Thomson, 1976.

Shore, Elliott and James Danky, eds. "Alternative Materials in Libraries: A Handbook," *Collection Building* v2 n2 (March 1980).

Silet, Charles P. "Annotated Checklist of Articles and Books on American Little Magazines," *Bulletin of Bibliography and Magazine Notes* v34 n4 (December 1977), 157--166, 208.

Sipapu. 1970-- . Noel Peattie, ed. Konocti Books, Rt. 1, Box 216, Winters, CA 95694.

Small Press Review. 1967-- . Len Fulton, ed. Dustbooks, Box 100, Paradise, CA 95969.

Stony Hills: The New England Alternative Press Review. 1977-- . Diane Kruchkow, ed. Rat & Mole Press, Box 715, Newburyport, MA 01950.

Swallow, Alan. "The Little Magazine," *Prairie Schooner* 16 (Winter 1942), p. 238--243.

Trace: A Chronicle of Living Literature. n1–72/73, 1952–1970. Hollywood, CA.

Tregenza, John. *Australian Little Magazines, 1923--1954.* Adelaide: Libraries Board of Southern Australia, 1964.

Union List of Little Magazines. Chicago: Midwest Inter-library Center, 1956.

Whittemore, Reed. *Little Magazines.* Minneapolis: University of Minnesota, 1963.

Zulauf, Sander W. and Irwin H. Weiser, eds. *Index of American Periodical Verse.* Metuchen, NJ: Scarecrow Press, 1973- .

THE EXCHANGE OF PUBLICATIONS: AN ALTERNATIVE TO ACQUISITIONS

Pamela Bluh and Virginia C. Haines

The exchange of publications between American and foreign libraries has been dealt with in the literature on several occasions, yet little has been written about the topic as it relates to current concepts of fiscal responsibility and collection development activities. At a time of austerity, it seems appropriate that the exchange agreement as an alternative means of acquisition should be reviewed and the philosophical and practical considerations of exchanges should be examined to determine if this method of acquisition continues to be viable.

In many libraries, exchange agreements have long and honorable histories whose beginnings are often shrouded in mystery. In the United States, the precedent for the establishment of exchange agreements was based on an 1840 Joint Resolution of Congress, authorizing the Library of Congress to exchange published materials with foreign libraries.[1] During the last half of the nineteenth century, and following the example of the Library of Congress, many academic libraries began exchange programs with foreign academies, societies, and universities. These private agreements served a dual purpose: to distribute American publications abroad and to obtain foreign materials for libraries in this country.

In examining exchange programs, one may note that their evolution appears to be closely linked to international political and economic developments. As the American position in the world arena has fluctuated, the status of exchange programs has also shifted. Depression, recession, and changing political fortunes have subtly influenced such agreements. If commercial and diplomatic activities ceased or were greatly curtailed, exchange relationships ended or were suspended. When activities resumed, exchange programs were similarly revitalized.

In the first decade of the twentieth century, exchange agreements were usually established on a *quid pro quo* basis. Immediately following the Second World War, a period which has been characterized as one of remarkable growth, international exchange relationships began to be formed on an entirely new basis. During the immediate post-war period, American libraries were in a dominant position *vis a vis* their European counterparts. The devastations of war and the interruption of scholarly activities experienced by European institutions did not occur here, and American libraries were in a position to assist European libraries in their major rebuilding effort. This assistance took a variety of forms, including the establishment of new and renewed library exchange agreements.

The expansion of the exchange of scholarly publications in the decade immediately following the war closely parallels international political developments. The creation of Unesco in 1946 led directly to the centralization, allocation, distribution and exchange of publications. Issues of the *Unesco Bulletin for Libraries*, which began publication in April 1947, contained lists of works requested or offered on exchange. In the United States, the Commission for International Educational Reconstruction and later the Advisory Committee on Educational and Cultural Relations with Occupied Countries, under the aegis of the American Council on Education, were, to a great extent, responsible for coordinating the educational recovery effort.

In 1948, as a further indication of the importance exchanges had achieved, the " . . . hope was expressed that Unesco would encourage the establishment in each country of a national office for the exchange of publications . . . . "[2] In 1948, the European Recovery Program received congressional approval. Often referred to as the Marshall Plan, after Secretary of State George C. Marshall, it was designed as a national effort to provide economic and financial aid to European countries. At the same time, the European Recovery Program gave impetus to the private sector to assist in the recovery operation.

> As the recovery program progresses, private enterprise will be able to play an increasingly important role. The Committee [on Foreign Relations] has been impressed by the repeated testimony which demonstrated that individual American participation in European aid elicits many responses of good will.[3]

These official international and national agreements stressed the need for cooperation in the recovery effort and set the tone by which institutions could participate individually. In the early post-war years, attention was focussed on providing assistance and on building collections as rapidly as possible. Exchanges that had lapsed during the war were restablished and new exchange agreements were actively sought and negotiated. Agreements with organizations and institutions behind the Iron Curtain were made during these years, thereby slightly defrosting the Cold War.

Throughout the 1950s and 1960s an expansionist attitude

prevailed, and many American libraries strongly supported exchange programs. In the 1970s, the special relationship between international events and changing patterns in exchange agreements can readily be detected. For example, exchanges with Cuba and the People's Republic of China, virtually impossible for many years, once again became possible and in fact are eagerly sought. With the easing of diplomatic tensions, cultural and economic ties are being reestablished and individual institutions send and receive material much more freely.

During the last 30 years, libraries did not concern themselves with an accurate assessment of the material received on exchange and they gave equally little consideration to a precise monitoring of the costs involved. Exchange programs were viewed in this country as a generous gesture on the part of affluent libraries, assisting those less fortunate. In the middle sixties, money flowed like honey, and libraries luxuriated in acquiring whatever was requested. By the early seventies, however, libraries found themselves ill-prepared to deal with the financial problems that began to manifest themselves. Substantial sums of money were no longer available and means to restrict growth and reduce spending had to be found immediately. Fiscal accountability and a review of acquisitions policies and procedures became urgent. Quite naturally, the exchange of publications was to be included in the review process.

Cost Effectiveness of Exchanges

The suggestion which is sometimes voiced that libraries receiving publications at a nominal cost for the purpose of exchange should not consider these costs in assessing their exchange operations are anathema, and totally unacceptable in light of the present economic climate. To believe that exchange programs are free is a fallacy, for the hidden costs alone must be considered as very real expenses. Furthermore, libraries in many instances do not receive the publications which they distribute on exchange on a complimentary basis, but must pay for them as any subscriber or subscription agency would do.

In many academic libraries, the exchange program centers around the exchange of journal material. Therefore, when the serials collection comes under scrutiny in many libraries, it seems reasonable that serials received on exchange should be subjected to the same careful evaluation as those received on the basis of paid subscriptions. The staggering increases in subscription rates are responsible in large part for the fiscal dilemma in which libraries have found themselves. Thus it is expedient not only to evaluate the titles received on exchange but, at the same time, to assess each individual exchange agreement.

Sentiment, which is often associated with exchange agreements, especially those of long standing, must be set aside and the review treated in a business-like, professional manner. It is no longer acceptable to enjoy the satisfaction of entering into exchange agreements which have little or no benefit for the organization and, although difficult to accept, it is essential to recognize that the most magnificent publications of the highest scholarly caliber, cannot be justified if they are not relevant to academic programs and do not support existing research needs.

Just as library management is a business that must function efficiently and effectively, a library's exchange program reflects that business in microcosm. Inflation and the fluctuating exchange rate of the dollar have combined to make it imperative that exchange agreements continue to be reviewed so that a monetary balance is strictly maintained; so that incoming materials continue to support the needs of the faculty and students; and so that materials dispatched remain within often stringent budgetary limits.

In reviewing exchange agreements and in making decisions about cancellations and retentions, a strictly monetary approach should be taken. The traditional reasons for initiating exchange agreements, the unavailability of a title on a subscription basis, or the exchange partner's lack of resources in Western currency with which to acquire publications, are now much less common factors than they were 25 or 35 years ago. For example, of more than 500 titles received by virtue of exchange agreements, only eight are available exclusively on exchange.

Types of Agreements

The framework for exchange agreements varies from one institution to another and may focus on the exchange of duplicates, gifts, or purchased subscriptions.[4] In many academic libraries, however, the exchange program is centered around the publications of the university press or of individual academic departments. It is clear that, regardless of the source of the documents being exchanged, exchange agreements must be viewed in a dual context. The fiscal integrity of the program must be a primary concern, yet, simultaneously one does not want to lose sight of the special value such agreements have that go beyond mere monetary considerations. The cordial ties shared by exchange partners make many agreements very special. Nevertheless, unprofitable exchange agreements must be terminated and the dispatch of materials discontinued if necessary.

Difficulties arise in dealing with some foreign organizations who are not as scrupulous about the termination of exchange agreements as American libraries and who continue, sometimes for years, to send materials. Perhaps the rationale behind this development is the hope that, one day, something will be sent in return. The receipt of such unsolicited material, which may stem from discontinued exchange agreements, could account for the very close relationship between exchanges and gifts functions found in many libraries.

Many foreign institutions do not seem to be as concerned with the costs of maintaining an exchange program as do American libraries. Frequently foreign organizations receive institutional and/or governmental subsidies to underwrite their expenses. However, from the American standpoint, an exchange program must be cost-effective and expenditures and income should be carefully balanced.

An important aspect of exchange programs, and one which received little attention, concerns the expenses connected with the transmittal of publications. In some cases, the dispatch is handled entirely by the publisher, and expenses for postage are thus subsumed as part of the price of the subscription. In other cases, the exchange partners themselves are responsible for the dispatch of the materials. It would be useful to examine our dispatch procedures and determine the expenses involved. If this were done, particularly by foreign partners, a reduction in the shipment of unwanted and unsolicited materials might take place.

At the international level, the exchange of publications takes place through national exchange centers which exist in many countries. These offices have been granted permission by the Universal Postal Union to transmit exchange materials between centers at reduced rates. In the United States, the agent for the international transmission of exchange materials is the International Exchange Service, located at the Smithsonian Institution. The IES serves as a middleman between institutions and the national exchange centers in other countries.

The use of the International Exchange Service for the dispatch of materials has both advantages and disadvantages.[5] As postage rates escalate using the services of the IES may significantly reduce a library's expenses, since the institution bears only the costs of shipping materials to the Smithsonian and all other costs are borne by the government. The savings realized by this means of dispatch may be offset by the fact that the IES and the other national exchange centers ship materials in batches, so that the delivery of materials is not as speedy as that of individual shipments.

For libraries who are unable to, or do not wish to enter into individual exchange agreements, a special program, sponsored by the American Mathematical Society, makes approximately a dozen Japanese mathematical journals available for a minimal handling fee. The only disadvantage to this program is that the titles offered vary from one year to the next and libraries may have to make alternative acquisitions arrangements as titles move on and off the availability list.

Beyond the formal acquisitions procedure, exchange agreements offer an additional sense of continuity and history which may be considered anachronistic in today's impermanent and future-oriented society. It is satisfying to know that even with firm fiscal accountability, amicable relations can be maintained and strong bonds of friendship continue to exist between institutions. Exchange agreements can also have distinct practical advantages. Exchange partners may make special demands on each other that would be impractical, if not impossible, as part of a normal publisher/library relationship. During the Second World War, for example, when it was difficult to maintain a regular flow of materials, many libraries on both sides of the Atlantic managed to store issues of journals safely and at the end of the war, were able to ship the accumulated backfile to their exchange partners. As a result, many libraries are fortunate to own complete runs of some of the most prestigious scholarly journals from Europe and America which would otherwise have been unobtainable.

Many of the reasons for entering into exchange agreements have changed over the years, and it may appear that the exchange of publications has outlived its usefulness. One must admit that the exchange programs of the past, with their almost limitless scope and noble purpose, are no longer practical. However, exchange programs which adhere strictly to monetary values and have established need and use as criteria for acquisition and retention, continue to find an important place in many libraries. If an exchange program is to be developed, maintained or strengthened, it is essential that it be totally responsive to the fiscal and collection development needs of the organization. Unprofitable or out-of-scope agreements should be terminated, but new exchanges should be considered and negotiated when they can be justified.

NOTES

1. U.S. Congress. No. 5. *Joint Resolution for the Exchange of Books and Public Documents for Foreign Publications.* 26th Cong., 1st sess., 1840.

2. United National Educational, Scientific, and Cultural Organization. *Report to the United Nations.* (1948/49):50.

3. U.S. Congress. Senate. Committee on Foreign Relations. European Recovery Program, S. Rept. 935, 80th Cong., 2d sess., 1948. *Report on the Committee on Foreign Relations on S 2202,*

p. 43–54.

4. Some institutions may consider their PL 480 obligations and their relationship with the Universal Serials and Book Exchange and the Duplicates Exchange Union as part of their exchange program.

5. Peter Genzel, "The Efficiency of the Transmission Function of National Exchange Centres for the International Exchange of Publications," *Unesco Bulletin for Libraries*. v. 30. (March 1976): 83–89.

BIBLIOGRAPHY

Akinyotu, Adetunji, "Serials Collection Development through Exchange: Its Relevance to Libraries in Developing Countries, with Special Reference to West Africa." *International Library Review*, vol. 7, pp. 503–514, October 1975.

Galejs, John E. "Economics of Serials Exchanges." *Library Resources and Technical Services*, vol. 16, pp. 511–520, Fall 1972.

Genzel, Peter. "The Efficiency of the Transmission Function of National Exchange Centres for the International Exchange of Publications." *Unesco Bulletin for Libraries*, vol. 30, pp. 83–89, March 1976.

Kanevskij, B.P. "The International Exchange of Publications and the Free Flow of Books." *Unesco Bulletin for Libraries*, vol. 26, pp. 141–149, May 1972.

Lane, Alfred H. *Gifts and Exchange Manual*. Westport, CT, Greenwood Press, 1980.

Lane, Alfred H. "Gifts and Exchanges: Practicalities and Problems." *Library Resources and Technical Services*, vol. 14, pp. 92–97, Winter 1970.

Samore, Theodore, ed. *Acquisition of Foreign Materials for U.S. Libraries*. Metuchen, NJ, Scarecrow Press, 1973.

Shinn, Isabella E. "Toward Uniformity in Exchange Communication." *Library Resources and Technical Services*, vol. 16, pp. 502–510, Fall 1972.

CONTRIBUTORS

Richard Behles is Serials Librarian at the University of Maryland Health Sciences Libraries. He formerly held that position at the Loyola/Notre Dame Library.

Pamela Bluh is Head of Technical Services at the Thurgood Marshall Law Library of the University of Maryland School of Law. She was previously Serials Librarian at the John Hopkins University Library.

Jennifer Cargill is Head, Acquisitions Department, Miami University Libraries. She is also Co-Editor of *Technicalities.*

Wilma Reid Cipolla is Head, Serials Department, SUNY/Buffalo. She also serves on the OCLC Serials Advisory Committee.

Mitsuko Collver is Head, Serials Department, SUNY/Stony Brook. She has published articles on organization for serials management in the professional literature.

Linda Ervin is Head, Client Services, Department of Finance/Treasury Board of Canada. She was formerly Newspaper Librarian at the National Library of Canada.

Virginia Haines is on the staff of the Acquisitions Department at the Marshall Law Library of the University of Maryland School of Law.

William Hepfer is Head of the Acquisitions Department at Texas A & M University Libraries. He was formerly Serials Librarian and later Acquisitions Librarian at the Pennsylvania State University.

Margaret McKinley is Head, Serials Department, at the Research Library, University of California at Los Angeles. Her other writings have appeared in *Serials Review* and *The Serials Librarian.*

Nancy O'Brien is Head of the Education and Social Science Library at the University of Illinois, Urbana-Champaign. She is editor of *Serials Review*'s "Media/Microforms Column."

Michael Randall is a Serials Librarian at the UCLA/Research Libraries. He edits a quarterly column for *Serials Review*, "Newsstand Magazines."

John Riddick is Head of the Serials/Microforms Departments at Park Library, Central Michigan University. He has also served as Serials Librarian at Iowa State University.

Cristine C. Rom is Special Collections Librarian at the Cleveland Institute of Art. She was formerly in charge of the Little Magazine Collection at the University of Wisconsin/Madison.

Minna C. Saxe is Head, Catalog Department at the Graduate School Library of the City University of New York. She was formerly Serials Planning and Coordination Librarian at the Research Libraries of the New York Public Library.

Steven D. Zink is Head, Government Publications Department at the University of Nevada/Reno. He edits a regular column on Government Publications for *Reference Services Review*.

RAYMOND H. FOGLER LIBRARY
DATE DUE